Beat Depression

Beat Depression

David Hinds

Hodder & Stoughton
LONDON SYDNEY AUCKLAND

British Library Cataloguing in Publication Data
A record for this book is available from the British Library

ISBN 0 340 78536 5

Typeset by Avon Dataset Ltd, Bidford-on-Avon, Warks

Printed and bound in Great Britain by
The Guernsey Press Co. Ltd, Channel Isles

Hodder & Stoughton
A Division of Hodder Headline Ltd
338 Euston Road
London NW1 3BH

To Tatiana

Contents

CONTENTS

Introduction

This book is for people who are depressed. It is written from the depressed person's point of view but provides insights and information for carers, friends and relatives of the depressed.

Let's assume you are depressed and in need of help. I have been where you are now. What you need is release: release from your all-consuming feelings of misery, hopelessness and isolation. You have just picked up the book that is going to make this happen for you. Life is going to get better and you are going to have peace of mind.

Chapter One invites you to take the first step towards recognising, identifying and gaining release from your condition. One tick in the appropriate box is all I ask of you. No matter how depressed you are right now, you can do it. Don't worry about defacing this book. These pages will have proved their worth when you are fully recovered and enjoying life as never before.

David Hinds

Part One

Depressed

1

You are not alone

I have been where you are now.
I will write for you and you will read for me.

Today is the day we get started.

Depression, like the common cold, is an illness that can affect anyone, including the rich and famous. One in five of us will be affected by the condition at some stage in our lives. Like most other illnesses, when correctly diagnosed, it can be treated successfully. Depression, although frightening, is never permanent. It does not reduce our value as human beings. Are you depressed? If so, how depressed? Let's begin to find out . . .

In order to ascertain the best and safest way forward, you must decide how depressed you are on a scale of 0–5. Your choice should reflect how you have been feeling generally over the last two or three weeks. Don't worry if your selection is not quite right. Give yourself permission to adopt a trial and error approach. We can always put things right later when we understand more about your prevailing mood, your circumstances, your feelings, your psychological make-up and the overall structure of your thinking patterns. Please go ahead now and tick the box below that seems most applicable to you.

☐ 0) NOT DEPRESSED	1) MILDLY DEPRESSED	☐
☐ 2) MODERATELY DEPRESSED	3) SEVERELY DEPRESSED	☐
☐ 4) EXTREMES OF HIGHS AND LOWS	5) SUICIDAL	☐

It may be that you will revise your choice later but this is a valuable starting point. If you have ticked (0) above, perhaps you are a loved one, family member, caring friend or professional acquaintance of someone whom you believe may be suffering from depression. If this is the case, it is probable you will read this book in a different way from a depressed person. You will be in a position to heighten your awareness and gain valuable insights to this much-misunderstood condition.

If you have ticked (1) to (5) let me begin by reassuring you. Due to a new generation of therapies and the widespread availability of non-addictive and highly effective drugs, the chances of recovering from depression quickly and safely have greatly increased. Your degree of depression will be dealt with in succeeding chapters.

Depression is best understood by observing its effects. The most obvious sign of depression is a persistent downturn in mood. Depression has a way of creeping up on you and dulling your feelings. You begin to lose interest in what is going on around you. You may feel sad, alone and isolated and cry for no apparent reason. You may assume a vacant, emotionless facial expression and you may feel guilty about things which happened in the past. Sometimes, with a different form of depression, feelings of sadness can alternate with sensations of elation or excitement, but this may be a mask for unhappiness.

In everyday language, we have a tendency to speak of feeling depressed when our transitory downturn in mood simply relates to a routine or minor setback – perhaps the prospect of returning to work on Monday morning after a particularly enjoyable weekend. On the other hand, depression as an illness implies a severe emotional disturbance, the source of which may or may not be traceable to external causes.

We all feel down from time to time. Sadness is a normal part of life. Happiness would hold little meaning for us if we were untouched by sadness. But when sadness takes an almost permanent hold of us and seldom returns to joy, the likely cause is clinical depression, also known as major depression.

No one is immune from depression. It strikes people from all social groups, all countries and all cultural backgrounds. One in four women and one in seven men will experience depression in their lifetime. *A staggering 340 million people are affected in the world today!*

The death toll from depression is formidable: more people commit suicide every year than die in road accidents around the world. Statistically, at least 10 per cent of the clinically depressed (whether diagnosed as such or not) will take their own lives. The impact of that one, irreversible action on their families, friends and loved ones will be enormous.

Let's make further progress by examining where you are right now. It will be illuminating and helpful if you tick the boxes alongside any of the following statements that you believe are applicable to you. Once again, don't be afraid of making mistakes and bear in mind that your choice should once again reflect how you have been feeling over the last two or three weeks. It is a general picture of your state of mind that we are forming here, not a medical diagnosis.

Much of the time, do you:*

☐ feel sad?
☐ feel helpless?
☐ feel tired?
☐ feel guilty about things?
☐ feel life is pointless?

☐ feel as if you are moving in slow motion?
☐ feel anxious or cry a lot?
☐ feel pessimistic or worthless?
☐ have difficulty concentrating?
☐ have difficulty making decisions?

Lately, have you:*

☐ isolated yourself from others? Or wanted to?
☐ lost interest in things that used to give you pleasure?
☐ experienced problems at work or in school?
☐ experienced problems at home?
☐ lost your sex drive?
☐ lost your appetite? Or gained weight?
☐ felt restless and irritable?
☐ experienced persistent headaches, stomach or back aches, muscle or joint pains?
☐ had difficulty falling asleep, staying asleep, or getting up in the morning?
☐ consumed more alcohol than usual?
☐ taken more mood-altering drugs than usual?
☐ engaged in risky behaviour – by not wearing a seat belt or crossing streets without looking?

Lately, have you been thinking about:*

☐ death?
☐ your funeral?
☐ committing suicide?

*Adapted from materials created by The National Institute of Mental Health, Rockville, MD, USA, and The National Depression Campaign, Westminster Bridge Road, London SE1 7JB, UK.

The exercise you have just completed can have the effect of helping to distinguish between depression and normal feelings of being 'under the weather'.

If you have ticked four or more boxes in total, the indications are that you may well be depressed. Have you been to the doctor? To avoid unnecessary suffering and disruption to your life, I believe you should consult your doctor for a professional diagnosis and opinion.

You know from your participation in the self-screening test what is likely to be the matter with you. Ten minutes with your GP will confirm or disprove this. Knowing precisely what is wrong is a prerequisite to overcoming any of life's dilemmas, certainly this one.

In Chapter Two, let's find out what is happening to you.

2

'What's happening to me?'

My mind is troubled like a fountain stirred;
And I myself see not the bottom of it.

William Shakespeare (1564–1616),
Troilus and Cressida

Depression is a disorder of mood affecting the brain and the central nervous system. In general, it is characterised by extreme gloom, feelings of inadequacy and isolation, and an inability to concentrate. The illness can appear mysterious, variable and elusive in the manner in which it creeps up and takes hold. It remains almost incomprehensible to those who have not experienced it.

Depression can be so severe that life hardly feels worth living and sufferers frequently feel unable to cope with their responsibilities. It causes a tremendous amount of misery and distress and is a major reason for people taking time off work. Even mild, persistent depression can take a huge toll on work and parental or personal relationships. Many people who kill themselves do so when they are depressed. It can be a potentially fatal disorder.

Other people may notice that someone displaying the signs and symptoms of depression is more inclined to:

- complain about vague physical problems;
- perform less well at work;
- seem unhappy, miserable and difficult to please;
- appear to worry or feel guilty about things in general;
- be more irritable than usual;
- seem isolated and unable to talk about things.

The fundamental cause of depression is a variation in the biochemistry of the body. Quite simply, the biological difference between having 'the blues' and being depressed is believed to be an imbalance in one or more of the chemicals noradrenalin, serotonin and dopamine. Normal functioning of the brain and central nervous system is dependent upon a series of neurotransmitters; these are chemicals forming part of the essential mechanism by which messages are transmitted from one nerve cell (neurone) to another, across the synapse (the space between the cells). This regular transmission of electrical signals sets in motion the complex interactions which shape our thoughts, our feelings and our individual patterns of behaviour.

Depression is an illness with a wide range of physical and

psychological symptoms. Loved ones, family and friends, as well as the depressed person, are anxious to know the cause of depression, but there is usually more than one reason and these contributing factors can differ from one person to the next. Simply talking about your feelings to a loved one or a trusted friend can be enormously helpful, however depressed you are, but the energy and motivation to put things right straight away may not be there if your depression is severe.

It is only natural to feel depressed in the aftermath of a distressing event like a row with our partner, a burglary, or a death in the family. Normally, after a period of reflection or adjustment, we work through our feelings about what has happened and come to terms with them.

It is at stressful times like these that our individual circumstances and our friends can make all the difference. If, for example, we find ourselves alone, in difficult or unfamiliar situations, anxious, physically ill, exhausted, run down, in debt or with other worries, we are more likely to succumb to depression, whereas in happier times we would cope.

This applies equally to children, teenagers and adults – male and female – not withstanding the fact that men find it harder to admit to their feelings of depression and to seek medical advice and treatment. In my professional experience of problem solving, responding intelligently to a dilemma that will get worse if left unchecked is not a sign of weakness. Just the opposite: strong characters like Florence Nightingale and Winston Churchill were no strangers to depression.

Personality is believed to play a part in depression. Some people seem to be more at risk than others. This may be due to body chemistry, or to the result of traumatic events from our childhood which have impacted on our personality, such as bullying, abuse, the various misadventures of youth or problems occurring later in life.

The genetic factor can be an important feature in depression, particularly with certain types of depressive disorders that can recur. Some people are more prone to depression than others because of their inherited genes. Until very recently, there remained a minority of depressed people who did not respond to the limited range of treatments previously available. The new strategy of multi-drug treatment for hard-core cases announced in the *Scrip Report* on depression and bipolar disorder (Scrip Reports, 1997) offers exciting new prospects of rehabilitation to those who had given up hope of getting better.

Our own thoughts play a major role in making us depressed (or otherwise) and this is one area of therapy where, in the course of this book, we can make tremendous progress in relieving depression. Later, when you are ready, we are going to shape and use one of the essential keys to release from depression, by using a system of revised thought patterns which will be fun and easy to grasp.

Understandably, when we are depressed, we can make the mistake of assuming that our feelings are at fault, when the real problem is probably the way we are thinking about life in general. Many of us, particularly those who are depressed, have a tendency to blame ourselves for everyday events that happen and to put the worst possible interpretation on things that are said to us. This misguided and rather selective way of thinking is self-defeating and further fuels our feelings of low self-esteem and depression.

To get better quickly and to enjoy life to the full, you will need to adopt a new way of thinking which is forward-looking and blame-free. In order to differentiate between the two ways of thinking we shall call the old way 'outmoded thinking' and the new way 'revised thinking'.

Fortunately, to master this revised way of thinking is simple. It will be easy, because you will cut out much of the stress and aggravation from your life at source, no matter who you are. Everything that is required for you to benefit is included in the chapters to come. A major purpose of this book is to help readers to look at their individual circumstances and to develop the skills necessary to beat depression.

3

'I cannot help myself'

The mind is its own place,
and in itself can make
heaven of Hell,
a hell of Heaven.

John Milton (1608–74),
Paradise Lost

The title of this chapter and the 'bottom line' are neither practical nor inspirational; they are defeatist. Why? The depressed person knows why. But family members, friends and loved ones, unless they have suffered the misery of major depression themselves, cannot understand why their well-meaning and genuine attempts to give comfort and help are sometimes ineffectual.

The tragedy of depressive illness, which, according to statistics released by The World Health Organization, will be the second-biggest health problem in the world by the year 2004, is that it can creep up without the patient knowing and envelop the individual in a thickening cloud of energy-sapping misery, extinguishing almost all of the joys of living. No matter how intelligent the person may be, depression can at times make it difficult to concentrate on even the most simple of tasks.

The mere fact that you are here with me now, sharing my experiences and reading this book, means that deep down you possess a courageous and determined streak that will help pull you through, even though you may be experiencing your darkest hour right now.

I am no stranger to depression. In my teens I was hospitalised for ten weeks with clinical depression. Throughout my life, approximately once every seven to ten years, I've had to go into battle mode to evict that devious, invisible lodger from my mind. In the 1980s and 1990s, when I was treating clients suffering from depression in my own stress management consultancy, I thought my own problem was history. How wrong could I have been? Nothing on earth could have prepared me for the absolute depths of depression to which I would sink in the aftermath of two paralysing strokes that occurred in the mid-1990s.

At times, as I struggled to regain perfect health in the years that followed, the motivation to help myself was simply *not there*. I could have read about the subject, but I wouldn't, not unless I could find an author whose experience was relevant to my condition.

I have been where you are now. I know the territory.

Please bear in mind that a sense of deep isolation is an almost inevitable feature of depression. Difficulty in communicating with other people, even loved ones, makes you feel as though there is an impenetrable barrier between you and the rest of the world. This book is a medium of communication. It is for you to decide the pace and timing with which you respond to my ideas and experience.

I fully understand that you may be lacking in motivation right now, possibly feeling fragile in the extreme and perhaps unable to make any substantial effort to help yourself. In view of this, *the very nature of your condition*, I will endeavour to make your recovery as painless and as easy to manage as possible.

4

What can the doctor do?

Healing is a matter of time,
but it is sometimes also a matter of opportunity.

Hippocrates (460–377 BC)

What can the doctor do? You might wonder. If you are seriously depressed and have yet to contact your GP as recommended in Chapter One, the chances are that you are not wondering at all. You are soldiering on in bewildered isolation under the mistaken impression that your troubles are yours alone. This most unfortunate state of affairs is confirmed by the Health Department in the UK. Their figures show that only one in two people with depression consults a GP.

Before I tell you about what the doctor should be able to do for you, please go ahead now and telephone the surgery for an early appointment (or allow someone to make the call for you). I am urging you to do this without further delay because I want you to be in a position to touch and enjoy the benefits that I am going to outline in Chapter Six. Doctors' schedules being as they are, it is possible that you may have to wait a few days for an appointment.

Do not allow yourself to be dissuaded from seeing your doctor by people who do not understand the complexity of depression. At a recent conference in London organised by the National Depression Campaign, it was revealed that the overwhelming view of the lay public is that their relative's or friend's depression is the result of money problems, bereavement or illness in the family, work or relationship difficulties. The importance of the underlying physical problems that render a patient vulnerable to these trigger factors has been seriously underestimated. Women, more than men, realise that an abnormal biochemical or hormonal balance may be the underlying root cause of the patient's depressive state.

These days, doctors usually have a range of treatments at their disposal including medical treatment with antidepressants and 'talking treatments' comprising cognitive-behavioural techniques, interpersonal care and problem-solving therapy. The term talking treatments is a general umbrella for all therapies which treat depression by exploring what it was that made a person depressed in the first place and what it is that is keeping them depressed.

It seems probable that the more severe forms of depressive illness are associated with chemical changes in certain parts or pathways of the brain. These changes are believed to vary according to the different forms of depression. Whether or not these chemical changes are the cause of depression, rather than one of its conse- quences, is not known. However, correct medical diagnosis and a sustained course of treatment with antidepressants can normally be relied upon to make good any biochemical abnormalities in the brain and to restore the patient's normal (or perhaps a greater) sense of contentment with life in general.

Typically, antidepressants take a week or two to take effect, although many people who respond to antidepressants begin to feel better soon after the commencement of treatment. Contrary to popular belief, they are not addictive.

The Depression Alliance, a British charity offering practical guidance and help to the depressed, makes the point that the most important partnership in medicine is the one between doctor and patient. Partnership in this sense means trying to give your doctor as much information as possible about how you feel so that the doctor can understand your situation properly. This can be difficult when you are feeling depressed, and the following ideas from the Depression Alliance's booklet entitled *A Guide to Help you Through the Misery of Depression* are ingeniously thought out and very practical.

Preparation for your visit to the doctor

- Before you set off for your doctor's surgery, write down how you are feeling. This will help you to remember important points and will also help your doctor get a clear idea of what your symptoms and feelings are.
- Sometimes it can be helpful to go to your appointment with someone you trust. You may be feeling very fragile and therefore be unable to concentrate on everything the doctor tells you.
- Mention your most important concerns and symptoms at the very beginning of the consultation.
- If you feel you might clam up (especially if your doctor seems a bit scary), write him or her a letter ahead of your appointment explaining how you feel. On the outside of the envelope clearly mark the words: *concerning my appointment*, followed by the time and date of your appointment to see the doctor.
- Be more concerned about your own feelings than the doctor's. If you are feeling pretty grim, say so. If you don't, you may never find out how sympathetic, supportive and informed your doctor can be.

- Follow-up is very important and you should always ask your doctor if and when you need to see him or her again.

After your appointment

You may begin to feel a little better straight after your appointment as a direct result of doing something positive about your condition. In the unlikely event that you are less than satisfied with the consultation you receive, don't hesitate to tell the doctor's receptionist, the practice manager or, if necessary, your local health authority. They may suggest that you see a different doctor.

When you are completely recovered and life is a joy once again (or for the first time in a long time, if you had forgotten what it was like to feel joy) spare a thought for your doctor and the level of service you received in your hour of need. Doctors can get depressed themselves and the occasional letter of recognition or thanks for exceptional service, if deserved, goes a long way to compensate for unsociable hours and the hazards of the medical profession.

5

Depression can break your heart

Depression is a risk factor for heart disease. Studies show that heart-attack patients who are depressed are more likely to die during the follow-up period.

Frasure-Smith, Lesperance and Talajie (1993)

THE BOTTOM LINE

Research has shown that depression and heart disease are common companions, each can lead to the other.

Research carried out over the last two decades in the United States on behalf of the National Institute of Mental Health and the National Heart, Lung and Blood Institute has shown that depression and heart disease are common companions. What is worse, each can lead to the other.

It now appears that depression is an important risk factor for heart disease along with high blood cholesterol and high blood pressure. In a study conducted in Baltimore, it was found that of 1,551 people who underwent tests, those who were depressed were four times more likely to have a heart attack in the next fourteen years than those who were not. While researchers in Montreal found that heart patients who were depressed were four times as likely to die in the following six months than those who were not depressed.

The first studies of heart disease and depression showed that people with heart disease were more depressed than healthy people. While about one in six people have an episode of major depression in their lifetime, the ratio goes up to one in two for people with heart disease. A recent study of individuals who were monitored after experiencing a heart attack indicates that those who became depressed after their heart attack are more at risk (Frasure-Smith, Lesperance and Talajie, 1993).

A large-scale study of European workers who had both depression and chronic medical problems found that when over time the depression improved, physical functioning also improved, as measured by there being fewer days spent in bed and less restriction on work and social life (Von Korff, Ormel, Katon and Lin, 1992).

How can depression lead to heart disease?

There is an ever-increasing weight of evidence to suggest that the presence of a major depressive disorder can suppress the body's immune system. Psychological distress may cause rapid heartbeat, high blood pressure, and faster blood clotting. It can also lead to elevated insulin and cholesterol levels. These risk factors, together with obesity, form a pattern of symptoms and often serve as a predictor of, and a response to, heart disease. Depressed individuals may feel slowed down and still have high levels of stress hormones. This can increase the work of the heart. When such individuals find themselves in highly stressful situations, the body's metabolism is diverted away from the type of tissue repair needed to combat heart disease.

All this makes for depressing reading, but already you have demonstrated a willingness to improve your personal healthcare by the simple act of reading this book. Very soon you will discover not only how to beat depression, but also how to reduce your risk of associated complications.

Exercise, of course, is a major protective factor against heart disease. Exercise has been related to fewer depressive symptoms in observational studies and it is beneficial and supremely therapeutic for those who are already depressed.

Fancy a break before moving on to the next chapter? What about a brisk walk or, if outdoors does not appeal, some press-ups, as many as you can comfortably manage?

6

'You mean I don't have to feel like this?'

If a man will begin with certainties, he shall end in doubts;
but if he will be content to begin with doubts,
he shall end in certainties.

Francis Bacon (1561–1626),
The Advancement of Learning

You have the power today to choose how you will feel. This book will give you the
means to use that power.

With the major advances that have been made in medicine today and our greater understanding of brain chemistry and therapy for the mind, it is no longer necessary to wait for depression to lift. You can take simple steps to start the process right now. The first step, which I trust you have already taken, or are about to take, is to consult your doctor and get the professionals working for you.

There are six steps to complete recovery and by the end of this chapter, you will be ready for the second step, which is to establish why you may have become depressed in the first place. As we progress to Part Three, you will learn to recognise and identify your particular state of depression so that you can familiarise yourself with the warning signs and take steps to avoid them in future.

Part Four is rather like a set of tools or a make-up kit – the basic essentials you will need to use or apply to bring about your recovery. In Part Five, you should be in a position to ease the gloom by engaging in one or more of the therapies that appeal to you from the range on offer. In Part Six, the final step in beating depression, you will have the opportunity to rediscover the joy of living.

Throughout the book is the central theme for getting better from all variations of depressive illness, namely the need to quit outmoded thinking in favour of revised thinking. To make this realisable for everyone, from a child to a pensioner, I have packaged the process into easy stages.

Depression means different things to different people. This book contains a full range of therapies available to a depressed person. Clearly, not all will apply to any one individual and you will be free to choose which are most appropriate to you and your condition.

A vital ingredient for your recovery is hope. Perhaps at this moment you feel recovery is beyond you. I will not ask you at this stage to be confident of recovery, but I ask you to hope for recovery.

'You can't massacre an idea, you cannot run tanks over hope,' said Ronald Reagan, fortieth president of the United States.

You have the power today to choose how you will feel. With hope in your ability to recover from depression, this book will give you the means to use that power.

Part Two

Why Me?

7

Inherited genes

*What lies behind us, and what lies before us are tiny matters,
compared to what lies within us.*

Ralph Waldo Emerson (1803–82)

There is a genetic predisposition to some forms of depression, particularly those that recur. For instance, it has been established that if one identical twin suffers from depression, there is a 70 per cent chance that the other twin will also. Non-identical twins, in common with other relatives, parents or children of a person who suffers from depression, run a 25 per cent risk of depressive illness due to the genetic factor.

The genetic factor appears to be an important one. Researchers on both sides of the Atlantic identified two groups of adopted individuals – those who had been diagnosed as having a depressive illness and those who did not suffer from depression. They found that the biological relatives of adopted persons with depressive illnesses had higher rates of clinical (major) depressive illnesses than did relatives of those who were not depressed.

How is it that our brains can be affected by the genetic factor to render some of us more vulnerable to depression than others?

People who have a greater biological sensitivity to depression than others are more likely to switch into depressed states of mind because something goes wrong with the way that neurochemicals are produced and used in the brain. This malfunction is believed to be due to our genes, the segments of DNA that control a vast number of chemical processes.

Genes are essential for life. They control the colour and texture of our skin, the face, the figure, the colour of our eyes and hair, and they bring about changes and developments within ourselves so that, as we grow, our sexual organs develop. Genes also play a part in personality and susceptibility to certain types of illnesses, including depression, but our individuality and the type of person we become mostly depends on ourselves and how we interpret the experiences we have had during infancy and early childhood.

The way the brain develops during infancy and early childhood depends very much on social input. The brain of a child who is loved and wanted might mature differently from that of a child who is abused and constantly threatened. Our actual real-life experiences condition the brain and this aspect of development marries what we perceive is happening to us in the outside world with what is going on inside our heads.

This may sound fine in theory. But how does it work in practice? At the fundamental cell level, a human brain might be compared to a computer. After all, computers are essentially a series of tiny switches that can be programmed for either 'on' or 'off', depending on the task to be performed. Likewise, our brain cells (neurones, to be more precise) either 'fire', discharging an electrochemical signal for some kind of action to take place (*run* – Daddy is mad at you), or 'do not fire', if no change is required (don't run – Mummy wants to give you a sweetie).

When, as an infant, you were distressed (as in the first bracketed example above), your brain chemistry changed to prepare you for the ordeal at hand, arousing tension in the body. Hormones such as adrenalin, noradrenalin, cortisol, and a number of different chemicals, impact together to affect the way transmission takes place in the brain.

Over time, and with repetition, these significant chemical changes, which occur in response to what is happening to us in the outside world, can have the effect of modifying our brain receptors and the kind of attachment that one nerve cell makes with another. There is a connection between the shaping of our infant brain and the outside world right from our very early experiences of life.

But what can we do to beat depression *now*?

Let's start with what we should avoid doing: we should not blame our parents for the less than perfect set of genes we inherited, or for the less than perfect upbringing we experienced as a child, even if our experiences were downright miserable. We can't change the past and our genes (some of which will be rather good and better than other people's) cannot be part-exchanged or re-engineered.

Blaming others for our predicament is one of the surest ways to stay in depression. In blaming one or other of our parents or anyone else involved in our upbringing, *including ourselves*, we negate our power as individuals and render ourselves vulnerable.

The future is decided by our current thinking. In order to break free from depression, it is imperative to believe that our parents or guardians were trying to do the best they could with the limited understanding, awareness and knowledge they had at the time. If there is something that you need to forgive them for, but you don't quite know how to go about it, you may find the next two chapters helpful, together with Chapter Thirty-nine.

The finest contribution to future happiness that can be made by the damaged child, cheated of his or her own childhood, and now in adulthood, is to ensure that the mistakes of previous generations are not allowed to manifest themselves in future generations.

8

Bitter thoughts

*If we could read the secret history of our enemies,
we should find in each man's life sorrow and suffering
enough to disarm hostility.*

Henry Wadsworth Longfellow (1807–82),
Driftwood

Forgive and forget.

Of all the quotations in this book, and I believe there are no fewer than sixty-six excellent ones, the one from Longfellow is the most telling of all. I am fortunate in that these days I have many friends and very few enemies. On those rare occasions when I look into the eyes of someone who regards me as the enemy, I remember Longfellow's words.

In contrast to many times in the past when I was prone to depression, I am no longer prepared to entertain bitter thoughts. I know, from experience, such thoughts do more damage to me than anyone else.

At strategic points throughout this book, in very small, gentle stages, you and I must work together to banish bitter thoughts from your mind and to establish a comfortable and forgiving environment so that you feel less inclined to embrace bitterness in the future.

It would be dishonest and unrealistic of me to think that I could teach you the techniques necessary to make this possible in one short (or extended) chapter. I can't. There are many seemingly unrelated matters we must deal with along the way before you can be expected to grasp that coming to terms with your past, and quitting outmoded thinking in favour of revised thinking, is the key to permanent release from depression.

Happily, we can deal with all of these matters within the pages of this book and we shall do so with considerable respect to your sensitivities. Before we can make great progress, however, we need to examine our own bitter thoughts and observe how we are keeping our suffering alive, red-hot and self-destructive.

All too often we perpetuate our pain by keeping it the focus of our thoughts, replaying our hurts over and over again in our minds, magnifying our injustices and vilifying the perceived offender in the process. We frequently add to our discomfort by being overly sensitive and reacting out of all proportion to minor irritations and temporary setbacks. How many of us have punished ourselves time and time again by taking things too personally?

Learning to exercise more control over our thought processes, and finding ways to neutralise our bitter thoughts, will give our brain chemistry a chance to recover from the ravages of yesteryear. Once we have mastered this simple procedure, we can heal the wounds of the distant or recent past and depression will lift because our thoughts play a powerful role in deciding whether or not we become or remain depressed.

How can this be? Quite simply, because our thoughts (those ugly, bitter ones, and any others you may care to have) come *before* the process of chemical change takes place in our brains.

We shall leave the mechanics of how we can train our minds to be more selective with our thoughts in general, and less generous with our bitter thoughts in particular, until you are feeling up to the challenge. For the moment, the all-important factor to embrace is that depression tends to sidetrack our thoughts and engulf them in one of seven downward-spiralling thought patterns. I have a tendency to refer to these undesirable thoughts as the seven bittermints, because I don't like mints. It would be a tremendous breakthrough in your recovery, and I would be so proud of you, if you were to feel able to identify your particular thought pattern from the seven bittermints below. If you think that more than one applies to you, select the predominant one. We will address your findings later.

The seven bittermints

1. Unlovability – e.g. my boyfriend/girlfriend/partner/date/that handsome stranger, etc. dumped me/doesn't love me any more/ doesn't want to know me. I am unlovable. No one will ever love me again.
2. Inferiority – e.g. my parents didn't care for me/I was abused/ abandoned/imprisoned/terrorised/they wouldn't let me join the club/nobody likes me/I have no education/no money/job/ friends/home/prospects/sexual prowess, etc. I will never be as good as others.
3. Entrapment – e.g. I feel trapped by my family/child/partner/ job/circumstances/age/state of health/environment, etc. I can't do what I want to do.
4. Failure – e.g. I didn't make the grade/pass the exam/get the place at university/get the job/win the contest. I was demoted/ sidelined/fired/made redundant. My business/investment /plan/ operation/expedition failed, etc. I am a complete failure.
5. Inadequacy – e.g. I am unable to cope with new situations/the new company posting/the new job/the new house/the arrival of my baby/the rumour that is going around about me. I feel

unworthy and despondent because I cannot provide what is expected of me.

6. Loneliness – e.g. I am all alone in the world now and I would like someone to care/talk to/get to know/come and see me/ share my life with, etc. What is the point of carrying on? I will never be happy again.

7. Dependency – e.g. I am addicted to gambling/the Internet/ alcohol/illegal drugs/other dangerous substances to the detriment of all else. I cannot control my habit.

> The bittermint that applies to me is number . . .

9

Anxiety

In the eyes of the advertising industry...

The most desirable mental state for a potential consumer is a kind of free-floating anxiety and depression combined with a nice collection of unrealistic goals and desires.

The New York Review of Books, 2 June 1983

Anxiety is fear spread thin and wide like a pizza.

Anxiety, the precursor to depression, can be broken down into three components. The best way to understand this is to imagine a cassette playing in a cassette player. The reel on the left has a recording of your past anxieties and the other reel, which represents your future, has only blank tape because you have yet to live and record the rest of your life. The cassette can be played both ways. Where the tape goes through the tape head is where you are in life now – depressed. Let us examine each of the three components so that in later chapters we can see how to strip anxiety of its power to torture and depress our minds.

Past anxieties consist of the things that did or did not actually happen to you – but you worried about them anyway, playing them over and over again in your mind, reliving and distorting the memory with every replay.

People who suffer from panic attacks or depression have a tendency to rake up the past and relive the awful things that happened to loved ones – or indeed to ourselves. We are constantly reminded of things we did, but shouldn't have done, to other people. We feel guilty, remorseful and wretched. That all too familiar internal dialogue within our minds consists of things we should have done but didn't, and things that we shouldn't have said, but did. Thoughts, action replays and voice-overs of tragedies and foul-ups in the past come flooding back to remind us how we failed and how hopeless we are.

No matter which of the seven bittermints from the previous chapter is your weakness, there are two areas crucial to your recovery which must be addressed: forgiveness and revised thinking.

By forgiveness, I mean forgiving yourself for past mistakes and forgiving those who have wronged you. By revised thinking, I mean the phase that follows clearing the mind of blame for past failures and the internal clutter that gets in the way of recovery. These two important topics are fully covered in subsequent chapters.

To continue the analogy of the cassette player in your mind, forgiveness and revised thinking are what will be recorded on the right-hand reel of tape (your future without depression). Later, in Parts Four and Six of the book, we have some unfinished business on the left-hand reel (your past) to sort out. In the meantime, let's ease our more immediate anxieties passing through the tape head with an excursion to Paradise Beach.

Paradise Beach

First, read and master the rest of this chapter. Then relax, take off your shoes and close your eyes. Become aware of your breathing and give yourself a few moments to settle.

Keep your eyes closed, but imagine what you could see if you were to open them. Fix your mind on just one object in the room with which you are familiar and explore its shape . . . its texture . . . its contours.

Imagine this object melting in front of your eyes without warmth or danger. Imagine it dissolving into white sand, crumbling under its own weight and becoming an assemblage of sand. Be aware that everything around your object is also crumbling into sand until you are left lying or sitting on an expanse of shimmering, white sand.

You are on Paradise Beach . . . a beach of soft, white sand. Towering behind you are palm trees gently swaying in the breeze. In front of you is the crystal-clear sea. You can hear the water lapping the beach and feel the warmth of the sun on your skin. There is a slight breeze keeping you at a constant safe and comfortable temperature.

Be aware of the sky above you with its fluffy, cotton wool clouds passing overhead and away to the horizon. Feel your muscles relax and become more flexible as you lie or sit on this beautiful island where you are alone and undisturbed. You are happy under the sun and enjoying the peace and quiet of solitude with only the birds to keep you company. Above the sounds of the sea, listen to the far-off cries of seagulls and experience the bliss of freedom from all your cares and worries.

If you want to, you can move into the water and feel the gentle waves pulsating against your ankles. Feel the sun penetrate your body, reaching deep into your bones, loosening all your ligaments and tendons, filling you with a warm sensation, calming and relaxing you.

Now prepare yourself to leave this place and come back to reality. Keep your eyes closed. Take a last look around you, firmly stamping whatever you see on your consciousness, so that you can easily return here whenever you wish. Slowly become aware of the sand around you reverting back into the shape of the object you originally fixed your mind upon. Without opening your eyes, visualise the rest of the room you are in. When you feel ready, gently stretch your body and open your eyes. You are calmer and more relaxed than you were before.

Say the following words to yourself with conviction, they will become true and relevant to you as you repeat this exercise once a day for thirty days.

'I am feeling calmer and more relaxed; physically, I will begin to feel stronger and more capable. I will gain more confidence and because of this feeling of confidence which I can feel in my very fingertips, I will be able to face things more easily. I will be able to do all of the things I need to do.

'I will feel this confidence welling up inside me and I will feel rested and relaxed. I will find it easier to concentrate and as I do so, I will feel a deep sense of security and comfort. I will find that my thoughts are less centred upon myself and as each day goes past, I will feel stronger in my mind and in my body.'

10

Losing in love

There are two tragedies in life.
One is to lose your heart's desire. The other is to gain it.

George Bernard Shaw (1856–1950),
Man and Superman

Life can be a *bitch*, but tomorrow may be a *peach*.

Losing in love hurts like hell and is almost guaranteed to induce anger, depression and despair. You may feel that you will never love, or be loved, again. You will, of course, but you cannot be expected to believe this for a while yet. The overwhelming sense of shock, outrage, disbelief, and heart-rending grief at losing your lover defies all rational thought. It shatters the very bedrock of your emotions.

This experience will humble us and we must learn to accept that it will take a while before we can get back on top and start living again. We are emotionally damaged and – just as if we had met with an accident and were physically wounded – it will take time for the healing process to take effect. In the meantime, we must take care of ourselves because we are fragile. We need special treats and plenty of sleep. In fact, we need and deserve an army of helpers. The time has come to be supported by our friends, who are so important they merit a chapter of their own later in this book.

Don't feel bad because you need your friends to help you now as never before. What are friends for? They are not only there to share the good times with you, as your real friends will be delighted to demonstrate. Just remember how good you felt the last time you helped someone in need. Surely you would encourage your friends to call on you if they were suffering as you are now? I, for one, am not too proud to admit that my closest and most treasured friends have seen me and comforted me in the depths of my despair.

Having been ravaged by two strokes and very badly treated by a woman – I think even she would agree with that – I believe that we benefit more from the painful experiences of life than we do from the periods of ecstasy. I was hurting as you are hurting now and, despite the apparent impossibility at the time, I have found the woman of my dreams and we are supremely happy. You will learn much about beating depression and overcoming the trials of life in this book. No matter how unlikely the prospect of future love and happiness might seem to you right now, I would expect you to be in a position to surprise yourself before too long.

In the meantime, since you're hurting so much already, I have no qualms about introducing you to yet more pain – aversion therapy – in the form of a rubber band to be worn around the wrist at all times, day and night. Make no mistake; used correctly, the humble rubber band is one of the big guns of stress management when it comes to getting absent lovers out of your life for ever more. Make sure it fits loosely enough not to restrict circulation, but snugly enough so it won't fall off. Every time you think of your ex, snap the rubber band! Snap it firmly so that it stings, but not hard enough to leave welts on your wrist.

This type of aversion therapy might seem crazy but it works. How does it work? Your subconscious mind quickly comes to associate the twang of pain from the rubber band with thoughts of the offending ex-lover. Your subconscious mind will, over time, short circuit the thought process to avoid the pain. Thoughts of your ex become less and less frequent and soon it will be time to cast off the rubber band and celebrate your new-found freedom with champagne and friends.

11

Career crash

It's a recession when your neighbour loses his job;
it's a depression when you lose yours.

Harry S. Truman (1884–1972)

There is always another opportunity . . . After two strokes, I know this to be true.

For just about everyone, losing a job or experiencing a career crash can be a shattering and soul-destroying experience. For many people, however, once the initial shock has worn off, it can be a golden (forced, unexpected, probably inconvenient, but nevertheless there for the taking) opportunity to demonstrate the strength of their character. As a direct result of misfortune or, in some cases, foul play by employers, millions of people the world over have found satisfaction in self-employment or been motivated to seek that special job that they might otherwise never have striven for.

Everyone recovers from depression unless, of course, one throws in the towel while gripped in the depths of despair. It might seem all-embracing while it has you in its clutches but depression, however frightening, is never permanent. Many people, when they beat it and return to the real world, are supercharged with energy and determination to change their lives for the better. This is the reason why we shall have more fun and make accelerated progress as we graduate to the second half of this book.

Think back to your schooldays. The general idea was to learn your lessons in class first and then be tested later. In the university of life things often appear to be the other way around. We are all tested at some time or other – during a career crisis or a bout of depression, perhaps – before a learning curve follows, when we have both the opportunity and a vested interest in learning our lessons so that we can end up benefiting greatly from our present predicament.

Hopefully, you are already on my wavelength because you are several chapters into the book that is going to help you to get things right. Here are some useful questions to ask yourself and to discuss with your family and friends. Be aware that your first reaction may be to dismiss the questions. It is not your first reaction that I am interested in: it is your second, third and subsequent thoughts that count. It is your considered opinion that I am after, and I know how difficult it is for you to give this when you are depressed.

- How many different ways are there in which I could plausibly end up benefiting from my present predicament?
- Have I failed if I benefit from the experience and move my life forward?
- Are there any circumstances in which one day I could conceivably

say, 'I'm glad this happened to me' or 'This is the best thing that ever happened to me'?

Believe it or not, I can honestly say that the two major strokes I suffered in 1995 were ultimately beneficial to me. OK, so it took me four years to make a complete recovery, but this tragedy forced me to review my life and change my ways for the better. I'm happy now.

12

Alcohol

Of course you can get a quart into a pint pot – you can get a couple of gallons into it, if you stay until closing time.

Patrick Skene Catling (1925—)

Many former alcoholics have found happiness without booze.

These days, there is renewed acceptance that some alcoholic drinks – when consumed in moderation – may have a part to play in health and nutrition. There can be no doubt, however, that heavy drinking and alcoholism can cause depression, serious illness and death. Sensible alcohol consumption to release inhibitions and to help get the conversation flowing at parties, etc. can, of course, be beneficial, but some of us may be tempted to drink to excess to relieve a depressed mood or to 'drown our sorrows' and that can be dangerous.

Some people who are very depressed and lacking in energy may use alcohol to help them keep going and cope with life. This might seem sensible to the depressed person but will prove to be a short-lived solution because any benefits from alcohol soon wear off and excessive drinking can so easily become a habit. Furthermore, there is evidence that changes in brain chemistry produced by excess alcohol increase the likelihood of further depression.

In view of the fact that many doctors who have questioned patients about their drinking habits believe that most people underestimate their alcohol consumption by as much as 50 per cent, I would urge you to adopt the sound medical advice outlined below.

- Avoid the temptation of using alcohol as a means of drowning your sorrows or lifting your spirits.
- Seek immediate help from Alcoholics Anonymous if you get frequent hangovers, along with the shakes, that are 'cured' by yet another drink.
- Get into the habit of sipping your drinks slowly and substitute every other drink with a non-alcoholic drink.
- Do not drink on an empty stomach.
- If you are hosting a party or an event, be considerate; offer non-alcoholic drinks as well as alcohol.
- Ask your doctor or pharmacist if it is safe to drink with any medicine that you have been prescribed.

Excessive drinking actually *leads* to depression more often than it is a *symptom* of depression. If you have difficulty cutting down or knowing when to stop, total abstinence may be the only sustainable option. Many former alcoholics have found happiness without booze, but not before they recognised they had a problem with alcohol.

13

All alone?

*Pray that your loneliness may spur you into finding
something to live for, great enough to die for.*

Dag Hammarskjöld (1905–61),
Diaries

Never give up hope on love.

The difference between enjoying the luxury, the independence and the freedom of being alone, and being lonely, is essentially a matter of how we feel about the experience of actually being on our own. Being alone by choice is beneficial to the soul; being lonely can be soul-destroying because it feels as if you are stranded in your own private world where only you speak the language and know the customs. You can see other people, you can hear their voices, but you don't seem to be able to relate to them and that hurts. It is humiliating.

When you don't bond with anyone else and can't remember the last time you shared an intimate look with another human being, you begin to feel the pain of emptiness and abandonment. If you don't have someone in your life who cares, what incentive is there for you to get up in the morning and do your best?

Perpetual loneliness can result in shame and self-neglect and eventually you start to wonder if there really is anyone in this world who will love and cherish you.

Almost everyone knows that dreadful sensation of being with people and, at the same time, experiencing devastating loneliness. There are many possible reasons why we feel isolated and alone when, in reality, we are not.

Of all the symptoms of depression, the sense of being isolated and cut off from the rest of humanity must surely be the cruellest. On the other hand, all the lonely people who John Lennon and Paul McCartney were referring to in their song 'Eleanor Rigby' were surely not *all* depressed *all of the time*? Some of them may simply not have had a partner with whom to share their lives.

I recognise the paralysing effect of loneliness and how it can impede recovery from depression. I shall help you through this difficult period in Part Four. The chapter 'Greater self-esteem', in particular, may be useful to you, but don't be tempted to rush ahead to it now. There is valuable information you need to pick up along the way first. In the meantime, please believe that loneliness is a problem for many people and it is conquerable. We shall conquer it. A chance meeting with a former secretary of mine certainly provided information helpful to me.

When I had been a partner in a magazine publishing house, my secretary was the most valuable member of my team. Whenever I walked into the office, she would immediately decipher my mood and determine, as she smiled and said, 'Good morning', whether or not that moment was the right one to present me with any bad news or tricky assignments. I always held her in high esteem (as indeed I still do), and several years after selling my interest in the business, I stepped out of a cab and there she was . . .

It was lunchtime, so naturally we headed straight for the nearest pub and got ourselves up-to-date with all the latest news and gossip. Just as we were about to leave, I couldn't resist the urge to ask her what she thought of me as a boss! At first she tried a touch of subtle diplomacy to side-step the question. I persisted, confident in my mind that working for me had been the happiest five years of her working life. Being me, I just had to hear it from her lips!

She sat upright and looked me directly in the face. 'Are you quite sure you want to hear this, David?' she said, sipping the last of her wine. Obviously, she wanted to tease me with some minor indiscretion, I thought.

'You are the most inconsiderate person I have ever worked for. If I hadn't been dating your partner, I would never have worked for you in the first place. Do you remember that day when I almost crawled into the office on my knees?' I remembered it well. 'I had a slipped disc and you gave me hell for being late. Do you want me to go on?'

This was not what I wanted to hear and it prompted me to reflect that maybe I had some work to do on myself. I never got around to it, of course, not until stroke time, when I was seriously ill, alone and depressed. That was the time when I found myself with the need (forced opportunity?) to work on my social skills. Strangely enough, my relationships, business and personal, seem to function more smoothly these days. You, too, will have your own opportunities to develop your new life and relationships. Who knows what satisfaction you will attain?

14

Perceived failure

Far better it is to dare mighty things, to win glorious triumphs, even though chequered by failure, than to rank with those poor spirits who neither enjoy much nor suffer much, because they live in the grey twilight that knows not victory nor defeat.

Theodore Roosevelt (1858–1919)

Failure is merely a detour on the route to success.

Do you, in common with most depressed people, live much of your life in the past? Do you dwell on past mistakes, misfortunes and mishaps, turning them over and over in your mind, as if you were stuck in a time warp? One of the most disabling beliefs that many of us have is that the person we were yesterday is the person we must be today, tomorrow and for evermore.

This severely limiting and unhelpful conviction keeps us tied to our past mistakes, our previous practices and our current limitations. We somehow buy into the convenient but fraudulent notion that history really does repeat itself, and that if we weren't successful in the past, we can't possibly be successful in the future.

This ridiculous thought is flawed. One of the most famous presidents of the United States, Abraham Lincoln (1809–65), illustrates the point. Between 1831 and 1860, the year of his election to the Presidency, he suffered two business failures, a nervous breakdown and no fewer than eight election defeats: one for Legislature, one for Speaker, two for Congress, two for the Senate, one for Elector and one for the Vice-Presidency. What is particularly striking about Lincoln's procession of failures is that they were public defeats – everyone knew about them, including his peers – and yet he went on to win the Presidency and, far more importantly, to prove that there is life after failure.

In fact, success often follows hard on the heels of failure, but the rewards of persistence are only available to those of us who are prepared to pick ourselves up, dust ourselves down, learn from our mistakes and carry on trying. Personally, I believe failure to be the greatest teacher of all time: she is not a kind teacher; but who can deny she is an effective one?

When your mind is full of confusing or conflicting data, compounded with the aftermath of mistakes and their consequences, your attention is riveted in the wrong direction and you can't see the right way forward. Difficult though it may be, if you can learn to lighten up in these situations, to laugh at yourself even though you are close to despair, you will free up powerful and potentially useful mental energy that can take you on a learning curve.

When we are able to laugh at our failures and mistakes, and at ourselves, we draw the venom from our own misgivings; we allow ourselves to become open and receptive to finding new ways of avoiding making the same mistakes again. Our fears, concerns and other limiting emotions dissolve a little every time we laugh and depression no longer feels completely at home in the crevices of our mind. Laughter facilitates detachment from the reality of apparent failure and presents us with a welcome opportunity to take a break and find a new perspective.

Understandably, when we are depressed, we experience great difficulty in letting go of our mistakes, learning from them, and moving on. Later, as we progress through the book, I shall present you with all of the strategies necessary to come to terms with your past, to learn from it, to kiss it goodbye and to move forward out of depression. Letting go of the sad things in your past will free you to pursue your dreams and rise to your greatest potential.

15

Dominant personalities

If I were your wife I would poison your coffee.

Nancy Astor (1879–1964)

If I were your husband I would drink it.

Winston Churchill (1874–1965)

If you are adversely affected by a dominant personality, master this chapter.

A healthy relationship, in which the participants accept one another for who they are and are mutually supportive, is the perfect recipe for avoiding depression. Whereas a difficult relationship, one built on falsehoods and unreasonable expectations or domineering behaviour that oversteps the mark, can cause depression.

In the ideal personal relationship each party starts as he or she means to go on – truthfully. In reality, what actually happens at the start of many relationships is that we put on our best behaviour in order to create a good impression; we hide or fail to disclose the darker, less attractive side of ourselves and throw in a few white lies for good measure. Although your partner may have embarked on the relationship in much the same way, he or she tends to assume that this is the real you and may, in time, become disenchanted and complain that you have changed, when in fact you have simply reverted to being yourself.

Those individuals whose wishes, hopes and aspirations are frequently frustrated, run a far higher risk of succumbing to depression than most.

It is recognised that relationships in which one person is the dominant partner can be satisfying and beneficial to both parties. However, problems arise if one partner is led to believe that he or she must behave in a certain manner. The submissive partner, craving the approval of the other, seeks to live up to the dominant partner's expectations and may end up feeling inadequate and depressed if approval is not forthcoming.

In my years of treating depressed clients in my UK stress management consultancy, I have discovered that if ever a case of clinical depression roller-coasted – that is to say, the client's condition improved, but then relapsed – the reason was most likely to be contact with a forceful personality.

How can a dominant personality adversely affect someone's condition to the point of relapse?

To find both the answer and subsequent release from the roller-coaster phenomenon in depression, we may have to gently but persistently probe the depressed person's background and upbringing, as well as his or her current and recent relationships, in order to stimulate recognition and identification of the relevant dominant personality. Once this problem is out in the open it is relatively straightforward to deal with.

Step 1: Think

Remind yourself who are the influential people in your life.

Step 2: The process of elimination

Make a complete list of all the people who have opposed you in any way, commencing with the most recent opposition, and then continuing right back to childhood. For example, a typical list might read: husband/wife, ex-partner, VAT inspector, bank manager, boss, landlord/landlady, uncle/aunt, doctor, father, mother, teacher, nanny. It could be that the list includes someone now dead.

Go through the list *deleting only one entry at a time*, commencing with the least influential and, therefore, the least likely to be unknowingly causing you problems. Repeat the process until *only one* name remains – there must be *only one*: the significant one. If there are ten names on the list to begin with, you must go through the process nine times in total.

Step 3: Dealing with the problem once identified

Sometimes the significant one is no longer present in your life, for example, an overly strict stepmother or an institutional care worker. Tell yourself this person no longer has the right to exert his or her influence over you. You can do very well without their approval in future. Later, in Part Four of this book, you will discover powerful new techniques that will enable you to disconnect from the past and move ahead.

You should by now be in a position to recognise with absolute certainty the person who is adversely affecting your ability to recover from depression if, indeed, you are one of the minority of people to be emotionally impacted in this way.

In the event that you are still confused, bear in mind that this process can be even more effective if you get someone you respect to do it with you, to help you with your responses and to acknowledge your identification of the dominant personality. Run through the process again, this time with the assistance of an unbiased friend or relative. This person should *not* be the dominant personality.

If the significant dominant personality is curently part of your life you *must* make radical changes to the nature or status of the relationship in order to get well and stay that way. In the event that you are romantically attached to, or professionally connected with, this person, he or she must be willing to respond positively to your sensitivities in future or the relationship is doomed.

In a worst-case scenario, if you don't get the co-operation you need, you should possibly consider ending the relationship or, at the very least, taking an immediate, four-week break from it. Why twenty-eight days? That's how long, after a trauma like this, it will take for your mind to rest easy and regain equilibrium.

This is a difficult process and you should feel proud that you have identified the person responsible for your discomfort and been able to understand how he/she has influenced you. You have to ask yourself why you allow yourself to be tormented in this way. You must work on building up your self-esteem. Value yourself more than you have done before. It is your life.

16

Debt, despondency and death

He who has never hoped can never despair.

George Bernard Shaw (1856–1950),
Caesar and Cleopatra

This is when true friends show their worth.

Is it possible in one short chapter to do justice to the complexities of debt, despondency and the death of a loved one, explaining in detail how each may impact on depression? No, this is not my intention. At this stage in the book, I wish only to acknowledge the importance and the significance of these distressing events in respect of your own depressive illness if, indeed, one or more of these factors are relevant to you.

Debt

Debt and money worries are a major cause of stress and depression and insufficient funds have wrecked many relationships and lives. Although having sufficient money to meet all demands doesn't totally eliminate stress, not having enough money to remain solvent is definitely stress inducing and liable to lead to depression.

Financial consultants recommend that we should save at least 10 per cent of our earnings. Apparently, we will enjoy a clean bill of financial health for life if we spend what we have left over after saving rather than saving what's left over after spending! It is never too late to get into the habit of saving and even those on low incomes can usually make economies if really determined.

If you are already in debt, seek advice and guidance without delay from your lender or an independent agency. In the United Kingdom, the nationwide network of Citizens Advice Bureaux can be most helpful. Here are their suggestions to help avoid some of the classic causes of financial problems:

- Except for essentials, try to avoid shopping if you feel lonely, bored, stressed or depressed.
- Avoid shopping simply for recreation purposes. Find something potentially less expensive to do.
- Shop only with a shopping list in hand and stick to a pre-arranged spending budget.
- Give yourself a cooling-off period before making any non-essential purchases.
- Whenever you are tempted to buy anything that could be regarded as a luxury, work out in advance just how many hours you are going to have to work in order to be able to afford this item.

Utilising this system, you may decide that you don't want to spend the money after all.

Despondency

Life for the clinically depressed, despondent person can seem like a life sentence of regret: regret for the lost opportunities and the mistakes of the past, regret for the momentum and enthusiasm that have evaporated from present-day life, and premature regret for a future perceived by the individual to be futile and already lost.

Given this wretched degree of despondency, it is hardly surprising that the depressed person's thoughts are permeated by feelings of self-doubt, lack of self-esteem and even self-loathing. In these circumstances, a visit to the doctor is essential before any major or lasting benefit can be derived from this book.

Death

The death of a loved one can be the most awful thing to come to terms with. Grieving is a natural way to release emotional feelings and it is our traditional way of making peace with whoever has been taken away from us. The process takes time and cannot be rushed. Many people choose a period of solitude as their way of coming to terms with what has happened. For others, equally devastated by their loss, the comfort of others is what is needed.

Family and friends can help to keep depression at bay by spending time with the person who has been bereaved. It is not so much words of comfort that are needed at times like this, more the willingness to be with them during the time of their pain and distress. A sympathetic arm around their shoulders will express care and support when words are not enough.

Grief is a process of adaptation and passes through a number of recognisable stages. These stages include alarm, shock, denial, anger, guilt (sometimes, but not always), acceptance and adjustment. People in mourning who become depressed are often having difficulty transcending the last two stages – acceptance and adjustment. They should be encouraged to refer to the 'Sources of help and support' section at the back of this book.

Touch can be instrumental in opening up the pathways to emotion and helping to release the anguish of grief. When we are trying to hold back painful emotions, we clench our muscles, locking in memories and thoughts that we have difficulty in dealing with. The professional touch of a masseur or a masseuse, in a relaxed and private environment, can have the effect of allowing blocked emotions to flow more freely.

The change of seasons can provide a change of focus and a turning point in your life. Even in the depths of winter we can see snowdrops rising from beneath the snow. If you have access to a small piece of soil and a few seeds, why not plant a miniature garden of remembrance? Many people find that growing new life while they're in mourning soaks up some of the pain associated with bereavement.

Part Three

States of Depression

17

Is this your child?

Children begin by loving their parents; after a time they judge them; rarely, if ever, do they forgive them.

Oscar Wilde (1854–1900),
A Woman of No Importance

A happy childhood for their offspring is the wish of every parent, but not the experience of every child.

It is unrealistic to expect a child, particularly a young one, to say, 'I am depressed'. In fact, the child who is truly sad is unlikely to be able to ask for help in any language that those in a position to remedy the situation can be expected to understand, even if they are prepared to forget their own troubles long enough to listen and respond.

My childhood got off to a flying start but crash-landed at the age of seven. I have fond pre-school memories of *Listen with Mother* on the radio and great affection for my infant school days when I learned to read. I was enchanted by words and stories.

Whenever it was time to go home from school, I would put the book I was reading into my satchel to continue reading when I got home, returning it to the classroom bookshelf the next morning before selecting another. One day, to my horror, a teacher pointed an accusing finger at me as I was stuffing a partly read adventure story into my satchel and scolded, 'David, you know you don't take school books out of school!' I can still remember the disappointment I felt at being deprived of an immense pleasure.

This famine in reading material coincided with a marked deterioration in my parents' marriage and I withdrew into myself. I left both school and home in the early hours of my sixteenth birthday with no academic qualifications. The following year, I was admitted to a psychiatric hospital for ten weeks, following an attempted suicide. I did not know and would probably not have cared at the time if I had known that I was suffering from clinical (major) depression.

Anxiety, depression and mood disorders are serious problems that afflict all too many children and teenagers. Sadly, in many but not all such situations, had their parents or teachers been more informed and less preoccupied with other issues, problems could have been identified and treated – and, in some cases, prevented in the first place. What greater gift can you give a child at risk of losing their childhood, than that of restoring it?

Even if they have the most loving and caring mums and dads in the world, some children will become depressed either through biological factors, traumatic experiences, or a combination of both. Furthermore, it is a fact of life that parents cannot protect their children from all the possible causes of depression all of the time, although much pain and heartache can be avoided with early recognition and treatment when depression occurs.

In childhood, young boys are far more likely to be depressed than girls. In adolescence, however, the reverse is true. By the time children reach their teens, girls are twice as likely as boys to become depressed. It is worth noting that boys usually show different symptoms of depression from girls: when young or adolescent boys get depressed they have a tendency to become angry, disruptive, sullen, even aggressive.

The indications of depression in girls of all ages are harder to distinguish because they can be confused with behavioural patterns which are sometimes regarded as socially acceptable: withdrawal, acquiescence and passivity.

The best defence against depression that parents can give their children is to provide a stable and loving home environment and to help them to develop resilience in life. Resilient children recover more quickly from frustration, disappointment, misfortune and change. They are less likely to be overwhelmed by the challenges of childhood and adolescence and, consequently, they are far less likely to become susceptible to depression.

The most practical and enjoyable way to help very young children achieve resilience is to take an active role in their development by becoming the person they speak to, the person who interprets their experiences, who helps them to overcome their difficulties. By responding to children in this positive, revealing and encouraging way, you assist them in fashioning and shaping the foundations for a flexible coping strategy that will allow them to bounce back with ease from the ups and downs of life.

Every child is unique. The better you know your kids – their strengths and weaknesses, their likes and dislikes – the more effective you will be in helping them to develop a coping style that builds on their strengths, and not on their weaknesses. Children who are encouraged to build confidence and self-esteem on their strengths tend to become individuals who can handle stress without distress and adults who can achieve their ambitions.

In contrast, children who are frequently discouraged or placed in circumstances in which they feel overwhelmed will eventually become discouraged and overwhelmed. They may retreat into themselves in response to their feelings of helplessness and insecurity. This can and often does provide fertile ground for high anxiety, mood disorders and, ultimately, for the onset of clinical depression.

18

Teen depression

We do not see things as they are. We see them as we are.

The Talmud (c. AD 500)

A wise and trusted mentor is invaluable right now.

Depressed teenagers need to have their feelings acknowledged an taken seriously. They need to be allowed to feel what they feel f as long as they need to feel it. They do not need to be told to sna out of it. Telling a depressed young person to grow up or not to b silly only serves to ensure that he or she will hide their true feeling in future. Nobody stays depressed if they can help it. It is the mo awful, empty, joyless existence imaginable. One feels isolated an in turmoil and nothing seems to matter anymore.

Teenagers who are depressed are often unresponsive. They fin it hard to tell others exactly how they feel, or what they want, an they seldom seem to have the energy to do anything constructiv One teenager, an intelligent, good-looking fifteen-year-old girl wit kind, loving parents said, 'I feel so lonely, so worthless, I don't kno what I want — I just want to stop all this pain.'

Typically, teenagers will fail to let their nearest and dearest kno how they are feeling and what might be of help to them becaus they genuinely cannot see how things can improve. They may on come to know what they don't want after they have been given i or realise what they really don't want to hear after they have bee told it. Rarely, without a wise and trusted mentor, do they discov what really helps because too few of those who care about the understand.

To someone else, the fact that they feel as they do may appea unjustified, illogical or downright ungrateful, and the depresse person may well agree. But realisation alone cannot stop the feeling the way they feel because their feelings are all too real. T attempt to deny how they feel is to deny them the right to the feelings. It is tantamount to saying that your opinion in a matt that you may know little about is more valid than their feelings. is this very same failure to accept their feelings that can contribu to depression in the first place.

Young people in their teens often assess their predicament, the prospects and their self-worth inaccurately. Based on no mor evidence than a foolish, unkind or chance remark, they may com to believe that nobody will find them attractive, give them a jo invite them to the right parties, etc. It can be devastating to teenager not to be allowed to dress and behave as their friends d and it is a supremely confident youngster who is able to resist pee group pressure.

Bullying at school or college is another source of depression. Students will undoubtedly fear the bullying, but they may fear the risk of reprisals even more if they were to report it. Most survive by looking forward to the day when they will leave or by skipping classes. Those who cannot cope become depressed.

A young person whose behaviour gradually changes, who becomes either disruptive or withdrawn, needs careful assessment. There is likely to be either something seriously wrong at home, or at school, or a real or perceived problem connected with a personal relationship. In a (growing) minority of cases the problem could also be linked to drug abuse or trauma.

If your teenage children are depressed, if you truly want them to confide in you, then you must be prepared to listen but not judge. Plan the moment, seek informed advice if you need to, encourage them to talk, then let them talk for as long as they want, for as long as it takes. After listening, gently probe, if appropriate, to make sure you are dealing with the real problem and that you understand it. Make your own helpful suggestions, by all means, but let them draw their own conclusions.

Your duty as a wise and trusted mentor is invaluable right now. Perhaps I have made this sound easy. It is not easy, anything but. If you are unsuited to the task, as many good people are, admit it, and seek alternative or professional help.

Simply placing a copy of this book in an appropriate place can do tremendous good should they choose to read it. You don't have to say anything, just do it. For your (or, with the consent of her parents, somebody else's) daughter, one single rose placed on top of the book will draw her attention to it. For your son – you decide!

Your role is to help them live through their depression as quickly and painlessly as possible and to tempt them out of isolation by doing everything you can think of to engage their interest, and assuage their discomfort, while accepting their feelings at face value.

19

Seasonal affective disorder (SAD)

Is it so small a thing to have enjoyed the sun?
To have lived light in the spring?
To have loved, to have thought, to have done?

Matthew Arnold (1822–88),
Empedocles on Etna

Tens of millions of people in the developed world suffer from a condition known as seasonal affective disorder (SAD). This phenomenon usually affects sufferers for approximately five months of the year. In Britain, this commences with the onset of autumn, around late October/early November, and lifts quite suddenly at the beginning of spring. Many people with SAD maintain that their feelings of depression seem to worsen the further north they live and the more overcast the prevailing weather conditions. Some experts believe that the very high rates of suicide in northern countries such as Sweden, which has the highest rate of suicide in the world, may be due to the SAD phenomenon. However, I have not seen any conclusive evidence to support this theory.

SAD symptoms include many of the usual symptoms of depression – decreased libido, lethargy and social withdrawal – and as the abbreviation of the disorder implies, sufferers feel sad most of the time and have little energy to get out of bed in the morning.

Many experts believe SAD to be caused by disruption to the human body clock, the circadian rhythm that co-ordinates our awareness of day (waking time) and night (sleeping time). The pineal gland inside the brain produces the hormones serotonin (the 'feel-good' substance moderated in treatment for depression by drugs such as Prozac) and melatonin (the hormone that regulates our waking and sleeping cycles and our reproductive cycle). SAD should not be confused with the usual winter doldrums. Some people with this condition may suffer insomnia so severely that they have problems trying to maintain their efficiency at work. Additionally, a minority of sufferers may experience a craving for carbohydrates and gain considerable weight during the winter months.

Unfortunately, spending more time outside during daylight hours will not necessarily bring relief to SAD sufferers. However, light therapy has been shown to be the most effective solution for individuals who find their moods fluctuating with the changing seasons and it is widely available in specialist clinics.

Therapy consists of exposure one hour a day to a 10,000-lux light box containing a full spectrum fluorescent or incandescent light, which can be up to thirty times brighter than standard interior lighting. Treatment is normally recommended to commence early in November and to end during the month of March, but times for treatment may vary depending on where you live. Be sure to follow the safety guidelines that your therapist will point out on your first visit.

For some SAD sufferers the condition is banished at a stroke by substituting all existing overhead light bulbs in the home with more powerful 150 watt bulbs. For safely reasons, make sure that all lampshades (which would be better removed in any event if they restrict light) can tolerate the extra heat generated by the bigger and more powerful replacement bulbs.

Finally, before concluding this chapter, I would like to touch on three further ways to help yourself get better: exercise, diet and winter breaks. The chapters on 'Getting active' and 'Food for thought' are particularly relevant to SAD sufferers with the additional recommendation that those affected should ideally exercise outside at noon (your lunch break, perhaps?) when the winter sun is brightest. It also makes sense to skip your annual summer holidays, if possible, and take winter breaks in the sun instead.

20

Internet blues

*Modern man lives under the illusion that he knows what he
wants, while he actually wants what he is supposed to want.*

Erich Fromm (1900–80),
The Fear of Freedom

Too much time in cyberspace is linked to depression.

Are you hooked on the net, depressed and trapped in a web of misery? More and more people of all ages around the world are discovering that the Internet can be an effortless expressway to information about virtually any subject – including depression. But a recent study in America warns that too much exposure to the Internet induces loneliness and depression. Worse, a BBC TV investigation into the Internet phenomenon screened in the UK in September 2000, revealed the existence of well over 50,000 websites devoted to suicide alone – some of them linked to those in suicidal despair themselves and hardly qualified to help others in need: the depressed, the vulnerable, and the potentially suicidal.

Many depressed people become obsessive in communicating their suicidal feelings over the Internet and they may even encourage others to follow suit. On the plus side, the Samaritans now have a sophisticated e-mail service and an on-line dialogue with them does help to reduce the sense of isolation and helplessness for the tens of thousands of suicidal Internet users who use the service each year. It also saves lives.

Researchers at Carnegie Mellon University in Pittsburgh, PA, surveyed participants' psychological wellbeing before and after a two-year study on the effects of excessive exposure to cyberspace. The findings demonstrated that those participants who had used the Internet the most showed the greatest mood deterioration towards feelings of isolation, loneliness and depression – even if they had predominantly used the 'social' components of cyberspace: e-mail, chat rooms and bulletin boards.

Internet users, particularly those prone to or suffering from depression, would be well advised not to spend too much time swapping e-mails and lingering in on-line chat rooms because it might well finish them off socially, as well as make them even more depressed. Further research in America indicates that millions of computer nerds, approximately one in nine Internet users, are escaping to cyberspace in order to avoid physical face-to-face human interaction at home. As a direct and predictable result, contact with family and friends declines in direct correlation to time spent on-line.

Kimberly Young, an American psychologist and author of the book, *Caught in the Net* (John Wiley and Sons, 1998), believes the Internet to be as addictive as drugs, alcohol or gambling, saying: 'In cyberspace, a shy person can become outgoing, a non-sexual person can be sexual, a non-assertive person can be forceful and a normally aloof person can be gregarious.'

Andre Levy, a London-based computer expert, says: 'People who use the Internet to that extent are living their lives in a substitute world, one in which they have no physical interaction.' Inevitably, the price to be paid in psychological and emotional terms must be Internet blues for some, lost and broken relationships for others and clinical depression for the most vulnerable.

The alternative? Live your life in the real world and use your mouse outside office hours only when necessary and in moderation, for a maximum of an hour or two every other day. We were born to *live* our lives, not surf the Internet. The computer was designed to be our slave, but so many of us are becoming slaves to our computers.

21

Depressed, functioning on autopilot

O for a life of sensations rather than of thoughts!

John Keats (1795–1821),
A letter to Benjamin Bailey, 22 November 1817

Depression will lift in time. The pilot will take control.

It is the experience of everyone who has suffered from depression that depressive episodes frequently vary in their intensity and these episodes may come and go for no apparent reason. The initial part of the depressive phase is usually of a reasonably slow onset, but in some more serious cases of depression, individuals can find themselves engulfed in gloom and despondency without warning.

As depression creeps up on us by stealth and silently takes us over, many of us tend to soldier on bravely with our usual way of life, denying to ourselves and to others that anything is the matter with us. We battle on as best we can, oblivious to the reality that the joy of life is gradually being squeezed out of us.

Sadness is always unpleasant but it is not as bad as depression. When we are sad, we maintain our self-respect, we feel better for a good cry, we confide in others and it helps. Not so when we are depressed: our self-respect fades and quickly deserts us and crying no longer seems to help. We feel alienated and alone because our friends and loved ones do not seem to understand how we feel and we no longer have the energy, the will, or the ability to explain.

All over the world, women have a tendency to react to depression more sensibly than men, even though a staggering 57 per cent of women who suffer from pre-menstrual syndrome have thought of suicide, according to a United Kingdom study in the year 2000 of 400 women with mild to severe PMS.

This up-to-date survey was conducted for the Women's Nutritional Advisory Service (WNAS), the results of which were published in February 2001. It follows the sad case of sixteen-year-old schoolgirl, Ceri Kimble, who suffered so badly from PMS depression that she hanged herself at home.

More than 80 per cent of those surveyed feel violent and aggressive for up to two weeks before their periods and a disturbing 92 per cent feel depressed. Up to 40 per cent of women suffer badly enough from PMS to consult their doctor about it and millions more may be suffering in silence. Approximately 3 per cent of women are forced to take up to two days off work every month because their symptoms are so severe. The WNAS claim that the best way to alleviate the symptoms of PMS is by changes in diet, nutritional supplements and an exercise and relaxation regime.

Whereas women who are suffering from a depressive illness may actively seek the company of other women for support, men tend to deny the very existence of their depression and withdraw into themselves, making matters considerably worse.

Another challenge to the medical profession is the 'smiling depressive'. This phenomenon is a variation of hypochondria whereby the individual at risk has rejected all depressive symptoms out of hand. Smiling depressives generally refer to their doctor all the aches and pains that are worrying them and then proceed to wave aside the actual diagnosis with a dismissive but valiant smile. Smiling depression is a form of masked depression and such patients often have difficulty in believing that their physical symptoms are the result of their state of mind.

In order for our condition to be classified as depression in medical terms, there needs to be clear evidence of a lowering of mood. This lowered mood may vary in intensity throughout the day but would normally prevent sufferers from being cheered up by their family or friends. This is the major distinction between being sad and suffering from depression.

When we are depressed we are largely unaffected by changing fortunes, happy events, or the efforts of those closest to us to tempt us out of isolation. Our mood does not lift in response to what happens around us. We have a tendency to remain in a state that is referred to in medical terms as 'emotionally flat and unresponsive'. Despite this invisible handicap, many of us, providing our degree of depression is not too severe, continue to work and go about our business but we are simply functioning on autopilot. We are not *living* life as it is supposed to be *lived*.

22

Clinical depression

In the real dark night of the soul it is always three o'clock in the morning.

F. Scott Fitzgerald (1896–1940),
The Crack-Up

Depression, although frightening, is never permanent.

Clinical depression is a disorder requiring intervention and treatment, just as any physical illness would require attention. Clinical depression, which is often referred to as major depression, a mood disorder or an affective disorder, is one of the most incapacitating of all chronic conditions in terms of social functioning.

It ranks second only to heart disease in exacting a physical toll, measured by days in bed and feelings of general discomfort. It is more disabling than many of the major chronic organic disorders, and its economic cost, in terms of lost working time and poor performance, is enormous.

Clinical depression adversely affects our thought patterns and mood, our feelings, our energy levels and our overall ability to function normally, as well as our physical wellbeing. It is most certainly not just a matter of feeling 'blue' or 'under the weather'. It's more intense than feeling sad or experiencing grief following the loss of a loved one and, most serious of all, there is a high incidence of suicide amongst the clinically depressed.

I would not wish the pain and isolation of clinical depression on my worst enemy, but if you are unfortunate enough to be suffering from this devastating illness right now, you will ultimately have an opportunity to get everything right in your life for the future.

As human beings, we learn very little from good fortune, power, prosperity and the easy life. The real lessons in life are learned through trial and misfortune, rather as you are experiencing now.

I learned the hard way, too, and although this may come as something of a shock to you in your present condition, I am grateful for the lesson – gruelling as it was at the time.

Now, instead of missed opportunities, broken romances, and shallow living, I have an enviable and sustainable lifestyle doing what I enjoy doing – writing! I live where I live because the people of the village are pleasant and I am not willing to move away to more exotic places. Despite my failings, ill health and mistakes of the past, I have found happiness and contentment away from the rat race.

Why am I telling you all this when you are feeling so miserable? Am I a sadist? I want you to know that the reason is because the seeds of my happiness were sown in the misery of clinical depression. The pain was so great that I decided to do whatever it took to get better and stay that way. Now you have the essential tools you will need to do the same, laid out in a book for you. Read this book carefully. I wrote it for you.

Later, when we have dealt with the mundane but necessary aspects of your illness and you are beginning to feel a little better, I will show you how to reach for your finest hour and put real meaning into your life.

The key to release from all that pain you have been suffering may be staring you in the face, or be inside your heart, or you may have to look in a completely different direction. Propelled by your eagerness not to feel as you have of late, very soon you will have the momentum to achieve the seemingly impossible and I will show you how to use that special brand of energy for your own personal benefit.

Clinical depression is a tragedy by any standards, but much good can come out of it if we are persuaded to put right what is wrong in our lives. Some people may see it as a signpost, a forced opportunity to do something else, something meaningful, with their lives. Right now, the only sensible thing you can do is to remain calm and focused on beating depression. In the closing chapters of the book, when you have absorbed all those things that you must absorb in order to be free of depression for life, your heart will begin to pound with excitement as we touch upon some of the distinct possibilities for happiness for you.

23

Depression in people with learning difficulties

Words may be false and full of art; sighs are the natural language of the heart.

Thomas Shadwell (1642–92),
Psyche

'I cannot express my feelings in words. My actions may have to speak for me.'

Some people, through no fault of their own, have special difficulty in learning to talk, in looking after themselves and in coping with life in general. The problem for many people with learning difficulties is that they are not able to express their feelings easily in words. They have little option but to let their actions speak for them.

Sudden changes in behaviour or mood, withdrawal, or not being able to do things they could previously do may be signs of depression. Unfortunately, it can be all too easy for the rest of us to forget that people with learning difficulties have feelings, too.

Although depression sometimes strikes out of the blue, the departure of a favourite and trusted carer can often trigger it. Sometimes one loss can lead on to other major changes. For example, after parents have died, people with learning difficulties are often moved to emergency residential care. This means they not only lose their parents and carers, but also their homes, their familiar possessions and routines as well.

It is particularly difficult for people with learning difficulties to cope with change and this is often when depression sets in. They are usually willing to work through their feelings about unhappy events and come to terms with them, but they will need special care and assistance.

Sadly, inexperienced carers often miss the early signs of depression and a deeper depression develops. Charities like the Down's Syndrome Association in London can be of tremendous benefit at times like these. They produce a range of invaluable leaflets for carers, which have been instrumental in the preparation of advice for this chapter.

People with learning difficulties are at risk of being neglected and physically or sexually abused, because they cannot easily protect themselves, or may not be able to tell other people what has happened. Abuse may lead to depression. If you are caring for someone who is vulnerable, watch out for the warning signs that something is wrong listed on the page that follows.

Guidelines to help carers recognise depression in people with a speech impediment or learning difficulties

- Sudden or gradual changes in usual behaviour.
- Seeking assurance.
- Avoidance of one particular carer.
- Loss of familiar skills.
- Loss of bowel or bladder control.
- Loss of ability to communicate.
- Outbursts of anger, destructiveness or self-harm.
- Physical illness.
- Complaining about aches and pains.
- Wandering about aimlessly or searching for something unknown

The above guidelines are in addition to other common symptom of depression which include:

- Showing little interest in activities usually enjoyed.
- Feeling tired all of the time.
- No get up and go.
- Eating too little or too much.
- Isolation.
- Difficulty in sleeping.

A number of studies have indicated that background music can be helpful in potentially stressful encounters, for instance, in circumstances when someone with learning difficulties is about to be introduced to a new carer for the first time. Similar studie have also demonstrated that soothing background music can be helpful in encouraging increased verbal communication. The indications are that music of an appropriate nature can enhance the relationship-building process and carers may wish to encourage depressed people with learning difficulties to participate in the music therapy exercise in Chapter Forty-three.

24

The 'baby blues' and postnatal depression

Baby, sleep a little longer,
till the little limbs are stronger.

Alfred, Lord Tennyson (1809–92),
Sea Dreams

The 'baby blues' and postnatal depression are two very different things. Let's deal with the easy one first. After the birth of a baby almost half of all mothers suffer a period of mild depression termed 'the blues'. This may last for a few hours or a few days and then it disappears.

A mother understandably feels emotional following the birth of her baby and can cry for no apparent reason. Some mothers feel tired and lethargic, others feel anxious and tense and tend to worry a great deal. These feelings are hardly surprising because when a baby is born sudden changes take place in the mother's hormone levels. Levels of some hormones required during pregnancy drop rapidly, while others, like those needed to start the production of milk, rise. These rapid changes are believed to be responsible for triggering the blues.

Rest and quiet are most important after giving birth but few mothers get either because they are busy responding to the needs of the new baby. The support and understanding of the father is most important at this time and visitors should be encouraged not to stay too long.

Mothers who have the blues should be allowed to cry if they want to and be allowed to express their fluctuating emotions. Plenty of rest is necessary. Should they appear miserable they should not, under any circumstances, be told to 'pull yourself together' and it can be a great help to the new mum if someone will listen to her and reassure her that her worries and feelings of misery will not last and that she will soon feel better. If the blues do continue for more than a couple of days then she should see her doctor and discuss the problem.

Postnatal depression is a depressive illness that affects one in ten new mothers and it can set in during the week of the birth and up to six months afterwards. Some mothers find that they are less able than others to cope with the demands of the new baby and they may be tearful, sad and despondent, or even downright fearful. Some may even experience pain for which there is no obvious cause other than, perhaps, anxiety and tension. Many have difficulty in sleeping and have a marked reduction in appetite. It is common when suffering with postnatal depression to lose interest in sex. This symptom can last for some time and it is helpful if one's partner can be patient and accept that normal sexual desire will return as soon as depression lifts.

Many women find that their depression becomes worse just before, or during, a period. An effective solution can be to ask your doctor to consider progesterone therapy to help prevent this severe form of pre-menstrual tension. At difficult times like these it is essential to maintain a healthy diet and vitamin B6 or a general vitamin supplement may be advisable.

Obviously, I have no first-hand experience of postnatal depression to offer you. However, the beautiful Iranian wife of one of my best friends, a nice guy from America, suffered from postnatal depression in a bad way. I remember visiting her at the height of her depression and being taken aback by the depth of her suffering. She is now completely well and a very fine mother to her son.

There is also a very rare form of postnatal depression called post-partum psychosis. Only about 1 in 1000 mothers will suffer from this and it requires immediate medical treatment. Symptoms include hallucinations, delusions, suicidal thoughts and attempts to harm the baby. Tragically, in exceptional cases of post-partum psychosis, which have gone undiagnosed, mothers have killed their newborn babies and/or themselves.

The most important thing you can do to help yourself if you are a mother suffering from depression is to believe that you can and will get better. Reading this book should help. Depression, however frightening, is never permanent. There are organisations and self-help groups throughout the world to help you through this difficult ordeal. In the United Kingdom please refer to the 'Sources of help and support' pages at the back of this book for details of the Association for Postnatal Illness, the National Childbirth Trust, and The Meet-a-Mum Association.

25

'I'm a man: we don't "do" depression'

Telling one's sorrows often brings comfort.

Pierre Corneille (1606–84),
Polyeucte

Depression is an illness that affects both men and women, but GPs throughout the world report treating far fewer men than women for depression. It seems likely that men suffer from depression just as much as women but because of their 'macho' mentality they are less likely to admit to depression or to ask for help.

Come on, guys, the game is up! We suffer every bit as much as those lovely ladies but because they are reputed to be the gentler sex, they feel able to put their tender hands up to depression, while we bury our heads in the pillow and suffer in agonising silence.

It is the way we often think about ourselves in matters of mental health that can be unhelpful. Compared with women, we have a tendency to be far more concerned with being competitive, powerful and successful. Most of us simply cannot admit that we can be fragile or extremely vulnerable. Traditionally, we have been conditioned to think that as males we should depend on ourselves and that it is weak to have to depend on someone else – a doctor, for instance – even for a short time.

To compound matters further, this traditionally tough and self-reliant view of how men should be is held by some women. Men can find that owning up to their weaknesses can result in their partner rejecting them.

Men, unless they have been specially trained, do not have the ability to cope with disagreements and upsets as well as women do. Arguments have a tendency to make men feel physically uncomfortable and they will usually try to avoid all manner of difficult discussions by making excuses or going out for a drink. Furthermore, men have traditionally seen themselves as the breadwinners and leaders of their families, but are finding that it is women who most often start the process of separation and divorce.

According to the Royal College of Psychiatrists in Great Britain in their admirable booklet entitled *Men Behaving Sadly*, men are around three times more likely than women to kill themselves. Suicide is most common among men who are separated, widowed or divorced and is more likely in someone who is a heavy drinker. We do know that two out of three men who kill themselves have seen their GP in the previous four weeks and nearly half of them have seen their doctor in the week directly before they kill themselves.

Men who are depressed are more likely to talk about the physical symptoms of their depression rather than the emotional and psychological ones. This may be one reason why doctors sometimes fail to diagnose depression in men. If you are feeling wretched, even suicidal, don't hold back – tell your GP exactly how you feel and then they can help you. Try to remember that depression is a result of chemical changes that take place in the brain. It is nothing to do with being weak or unmanly.

Many men who recover from depression, including myself, emerge stronger and better able to cope than before. You may see situations and relationships more clearly when you are better and find the strength and the wisdom to make important decisions and changes that perhaps you were avoiding before. Depression in men can have a happy resolution and I will show you effective techniques for beating depression as we progress through the book.

26

Depression in terminal illness

Can I see another's woe,
And not be in sorrow too.
Can I see another's grief,
And not seek for kind relief.

William Blake (1757–1827),
Songs of Innocence

Why do some patients recover from critical conditions when their doctors believe there is no hope of recovery? What do survivors do that makes the difference between life and death?

Bernie Siegel, the American physician and author of the book, *Love, Medicine and Miracles* (Random House Inc., 1986), observed that many patients who were ultimately successful in recovering from advanced stages of cancer had been described by doctors and nursing staff as 'difficult patients'. He says that whenever he consults on a case he is encouraged to see in a patient's medical notes entries such as: 'unco-operative', 'questions why tests are ordered', 'demands to be informed about test results' and 'insists on explanations about treatments'.

Siegel, as a result of his work with cancer patients, is convinced that terminal patients who get better instead of dying react to their prognosis as a 'wake-up call' to their very existence. They make far-reaching changes in how they think, act, talk and feel: reforming their eating and social habits and spending every waking hour masterminding their own recovery.

Siegel believes there are three categories of terminal patients: he estimates that around 15 to 20 per cent at some level of consciousness wish to die and will probably do so no matter how excellent their treatment. About 60 to 70 per cent passively co-operate with their doctors in every respect and will do whatever they are told to do, including dying when predicted if that is the doctor's prognosis. Around 15 to 20 per cent are exceptional patients. They reject the probability of becoming a statistic and refuse to be discouraged by the odds against survival.

On the day of the UK launch of my first health book, *After Stroke*, I appeared on the ITV network programme *This Morning* with Richard and Judy. In the live television phone-in that followed our discussion on the book and serious illness, a woman who had been told by doctors seven years previously that she had a life expectancy of two weeks due to cancer which had been deemed inoperable, phoned in to tell us that she was very much alive and kicking.

The show's joint host, Richard Madeley, in his own inimitable style, asked her, 'Why are you not dead? How come the "Grim Reaper" didn't get you?'

It transpired that her story had a lot in common with the views of many leading doctors and psychologists: survivors are not easy patients. She had been defiant, angry, indignant and not at all ready to die. By her own admission, she was not an easy patient and refused to accept the prognosis of imminent death. She used her anger (which sets off the stress hormones adrenalin, noradrenalin and cortisol, arousing tension in the body) to fuel her desperate quest to find a way, *any way*, of cheating death. She resorted to praying, healthy eating, positive thinking and self-talk (convincing her mind, body and soul that she really was defeating her cancer), plus just about anything else that she could think of. Even the most sceptical of readers must concede that something must have worked because she is still here with us now, fit and well and cancer-free.

In essence, she showed herself to be willing to adopt and utilise any possible action or reaction to aid her recovery. She expected to be able to influence events concerning her own body in a way that would lead to a satisfactory outcome and she was proved right.

I can relate to her recovery. In 1995, after two strokes and a subclavian bypass operation, I remember staring up at the ceiling from my hospital bed, partly paralysed and unable to comprehend the words of a newspaper, thinking: 'Is this me? . . . Yes it is, but I'll be back!'

I promised myself there and then that I would reclaim every single one of my faculties and then write a book based on my experiences. It took me many years but I made good on all aspects of that promise. Sir Peter Morris, Nuffield Professor of Surgery at the University of Oxford, carried out my operation and was generous enough to write a foreword to the book, in which he quoted an entry made in my medical records by nursing staff: 'He is extremely angry about his condition and shows this in his relationships with his carers.'

These difficult patients question why alternative treatments are not being offered and may insist that their doctor try something different. They are patients with 'an attitude' fuelled by the unshakeable will to get well. They hold the view that although they need the expertise and care of their doctor, they are very much in charge of themselves and this is not necessarily an attitude that all doctors fully understand or are equipped to deal with.

At this point, we need to make an important distinction between the terminally ill and the seriously ill patient. The information in this chapter is intended primarily for the terminally ill patient who may feel defeated and depressed but who really wants to live. The advice I would offer to any seriously ill, but not terminally ill, patient, would be very different: I would stress the need to relax, keep calm and to take things easy; co-operating fully with the medical team in order to secure the best possible recovery available to them.

There are tens of thousands of people alive and kicking and enjoying their lives today who were not expected to live or to make a 100 per cent recovery. Because of limited space in this chapter, you have read about only two. If, despite all, you still possess the will to live, why not give recovery all you have got and then some? It seems to me that you have everything to gain and nothing to lose. Don't worry about being a less than perfect patient: doctors and nursing staff harbour a secret admiration for survivors and so do I.

Is it possible for doctors to be right on every occasion when they predict life or death? Sometimes the terminally ill patient survives! Can you steel yourself to believe that the doctor could be wrong in your case and fight to live?

27

Retired, on the scrap heap, depressed

I love everything that's old: old friends, old times,
old manners, old books, old wines.

Oliver Goldsmith (1728–74),
She Stoops to Conquer

It is better to wear out than to rust out.

Retirement can pose a tremendous problem for people who relied upon their job to give them purpose and structure in life. Except for those people who relish the prospect of retirement and have many other interests or projects in mind, retirement, when it comes, can seem bleak and unstructured. Many retirees miss going to work, they miss their workmates and they find themselves wondering how everybody is coping without them. Sooner or later, they are forced to conclude that their former colleagues are probably managing perfectly well without them and that realisation brings with it a certain emptiness: a chilling awareness of being destined for the scrap heap.

According to a MORI poll commissioned by the UK charity, Help the Aged, in association with British Gas and conducted nationwide during the year 2000, old people in Britain are facing an epidemic of loneliness and isolation. More than a million of those over sixty-five revealed that they felt trapped in their own homes. Even more disturbing is the revelation that no fewer than 18 per cent of them say they have gone *for a whole week* without speaking to friends, neighbours or family.

Mervyn Kohler, head of policy at Help the Aged, said, 'This survey graphically illustrates the sheer scale of the terrible loneliness and isolation felt by many older people in Britain.'

You shouldn't feel lonely, isolated or depressed just because you are old. If you feel this way, don't hesitate: contact your doctor, your Social Services department, or the local or regional office of Help the Aged, and ask for help. Despite evidence to the contrary, this is still a caring country and there is someone sitting behind a desk right now (or there will be at 9 a.m.) waiting to help you. With the best will in the world, they can't tell you about the wonderful initiatives and opportunities available to you to meet socially with others unless they are made aware of your predicament.

In my experience of working with the older generation as a stress management consultant, they are a wily lot; they have known tough times before! Once they have been given sound advice and pointed in the direction of a solution, they can often steal a march on their younger counterparts because they have recourse to a lifetime of wisdom and experience.

Do make the effort to get out whenever you can. I know it can be difficult when you are old because of physical problems like stiff joints or swollen ankles, but it is worthwhile. Staying at home all the time can make you brood on things. This really doesn't help and actually makes you feel more helpless and depressed. So, whenever neighbours, family, friends, charity workers or the local community warden offer assistance, let them help you to get out. Even if you are not interested in making new friends, it is a good idea to have some diversity and excitement in your life to keep boredom at bay. If you go to a day centre, they may have their own transport that you can use. Above all, be open to new possibilities.

My aunt Freda, crippled at birth and born with no neck, has lived alone in north London ever since the death of my grandmother. I am not aware that she has ever had a partner – not until a few years ago that is, at the age of seventy-nine – when a retired British Army captain stopped her in the street and offered to carry her bag of shopping for her.

Instead of instinctively saying, 'No, thank you', she studied him, smiled her lovely smile and said, 'Yes, please.' This simple act of chivalry marked the beginning of the most wonderful period in her life until, sadly, last year, Robert died. My aunt, for the first time in her life, had discovered the joy of love and her life is richer and more meaningful for the experience. She has fond and happy memories of their short time together that sustain her to this day.

So, the recipe for a happy retirement is to gently bring to a close your previous working life (unless you can benefit from it from home, of course), be open to new possibilities and move on. This doesn't mean you can't remember your achievements with pride and enjoy thinking and talking about the old times. It just means you mustn't allow yourself to be frozen into your former working life.

28

Depression requiring specialist intervention

*I do not know whether I was then a man dreaming
I was a butterfly, or whether I am now a butterfly
dreaming I am a man.*

Chuang-Tzu (396–289 BC)

Be sure to take any medications prescribed.

The term 'clinical depression' is used to categorise any form of depression where symptoms are severe and lasting enough to require treatment. The general advice and guidance in this book is believed to be suitable for those suffering from any depressive disorder, however mild or severe the symptoms. There are, however, some forms of depression that exceed the scope of this book and those afflicted will require specialist medical intervention. Brief descriptions of these conditions follow:

Melancholic depression is a severe form of clinical depression in which the patient has lost virtually all interest in the activities of life and does not respond positively – even temporarily – when something good happens. Quite simply, the patient has lost the ability to experience pleasure. By contrast, most people with severe clinical depression can usually be cheered up by good news – albeit temporarily.

Manic-depressive psychosis is a condition that takes the form of alternating periods of extreme melancholia and equally extreme periods of elation and excitement. A more technical term used to describe some patients who typify many aspects of this diverse and complex category is 'bi-polar affective disorder'.

The manic element of the disorder is an abnormal exaggeration of the feelings of elation and excitement that we all experience from time to time. Some notable writers, artists and composers are believed to have suffered from this condition, including Ernest Hemingway, Charles Dickens, Virginia Woolf, Mark Twain, Beethoven, Van Gogh and Mahler.

When someone is experiencing a manic episode for the first time, the person concerned may not realise that there is anything abnormal in his or her behaviour. It is often a family member, a friend or colleague, who is the first to notice that something is not quite right.

Atypical depression, which usually starts in adolescence and can be persistent rather than periodic, turns the typical symptoms of depression upside down. While people with most types of depression have a tendency to sleep and eat less than normal, patients with this kind of depression tend to oversleep, over-eat and gain weight rapidly. They can be very sensitive to rejection, particularly romantic rejection.

Schizophrenia is a serious mental illness that affects 1 per cent of the global population. There is abundant scientific evidence (though as yet no conclusive proof) to suggest that faulty genes may contribute to the onset of the illness. The illness generally becomes apparent in the sufferer's late teens or early twenties – although it can be middle age or even later before symptoms become apparent. Patients are usually advised, because of the risk of repeated episodes, to continue taking medication for many years, perhaps for the rest of their lives.

Sadly, schizophrenia causes tremendous difficulty and distress for the afflicted and their families. Not only do sufferers have to contend with the likelihood of hallucinations, delusions and interruptions to their train of thought, they also have to live with the image of a deranged killer as portrayed in so many films and TV programmes – a representation which is far from typical.

One point concerning depression of any type should be noted above all others. No less an authority than the *Oxford Companion to the Mind*, advises, 'All persons suffering from depression should be adequately assessed for the risk of suicide. Relatives, and some physicians, sometimes hesitate to enquire directly about suicidal thoughts lest such questions prompt the actions they are most anxious to prevent.'

The evidence is that most depressed patients answer truthfully to enquiries of this kind and may even be relieved by the opportunity to discuss their innermost feelings of despair and dread of the future.

29

Suicidal tendencies

*My fortune somewhat resembled that of a person who should
entertain an idea of committing suicide, and, altogether
beyond his hopes, meet with the good hap to be murdered.*

Nathaniel Hawthorne (1804–64),
The Custom House

We only die once; and it's for such a long, long time . . .

I attempted suicide in my teens. I was led to believe that I was not an easy child and I should imagine there is much truth in that. My father suffers from depression and my grandfather, so I was told, had been depressed for much of his life. My uncle had attempted suicide early in life. Sadly, his only son did commit suicide early in life and my uncle has been devastated ever since.

I left home, school and London aged sixteen, following major disagreements at home. I didn't bother to take any exams or complete the academic year. On reflection, one or two of the teachers at my school, particularly my mathematics teacher, were supportive and tried to help me. I think they suspected there had been something the matter with me for years, but I could not bring myself to communicate with anyone beyond a certain no-go level.

I moved to Liverpool, working in a camera shop in the city centre and living across the Mersey on the Wirral in a youth hostel. For a reason that might seem inconsequential and incomprehensibly minor to anyone not consumed by depression, I decided to kill myself because I didn't have enough money to pay the rent.

I went to the doctor and extracted a prescription for sleeping pills from him. He was most sympathetic and reached for his pen without too much hesitation when I told him that I hadn't been able to sleep ever since my sister had been killed in a car crash (she hadn't).

On my way back from the chemist, I went in to a sweet shop and spent the remainder of my money on a giant-size packet of liquorice allsorts which I consumed with relish – particularly the round pink and yellow coconut ones with liquorice in the middle – along with the entire pack of sleeping pills. There was no suicide note. I had nothing to say to anyone. I had no regrets, no second thoughts, and soon afterwards, no thoughts at all.

The next thing I knew, there was a group of doctors and nurses around me. 'Can you see us? Can you see us? Can you see anything at all?'

The reason for their concern became apparent when I had recovered sufficiently to look at myself in a mirror. My eyes were nowhere to be seen. All that was visible when they were open were two slits where my eyes used to be.

Adults and children who commit suicide are typically those who feel that death is the only way of escaping from what seems to them an impossible life without hope, although, in some cases, it is a threat or a cry for help that went unheeded. The decision to commit suicide and the actions taken towards that intention are invariably the consequences of negative thinking – the primary characteristic of depression.

Suicide is still rare in children under the age of twelve. However, the rate of suicide among teenagers has trebled in the last thirty years. Suicide has now become the second highest cause of death among older teenagers in England, the United States and Sweden. The risk of actual suicide in the year following a previous attempt is nearly one hundred times greater than that in the general population.

More people commit suicide today than die in road accidents. This cannot go on. We have to embrace the skills necessary to cope with life in the modern world. We can start now. By 'we' I mean you and me. It is easier for me these days: I have learned to stop the negative thoughts that feed depression at source. With your help, I can show you how to do the same. Read on, the good bits are yet to come.

> *Die, my dear doctor? That's the last thing I shall do.*
>
> Lord Palmerston (1784–1865)

Part Four

Means of Recovery

30

Dumping excess baggage

How many things I can do without!

Socrates (c. 470–399 BC)

You can learn to let go of your bitter memories, your prejudices and your bad habits.

To bring about complete and lasting recovery from depression, you will need the freedom to open up new lines of communication between your mind, body and spirit. This will prove to be an exciting learning curve.

Before we can realistically move forward out of depression and stay that way, most of us have some excess baggage to dump. The baggage I am referring to is personal, very personal indeed: those aspects of an individual's character that manifest themselves as bad habits, prejudices, self-destructive thoughts and patterns of behaviour. These are personal liabilities we can live without and they may well have been a contributing factor in the onset of depression in the first place.

How did we acquire these and what must we do to dump them?

For the answer we invariably have to look back to our formative years. The foundation of almost every non-hereditary characteristic we possess, good and bad, stems from our childhood conditioning. Our parents and guardians start out with the best of intentions, of course, but few of them are experts in the art of raising children and many of them make mistakes, the ramifications of which may be felt by their offspring for a lifetime. Unless, later in life, one decides to put matters right once and for all – and that is where you are now. Never mind that you are not to blame – be magnanimous – take the responsibility upon yourself to do what needs to be done. The challenge to become yourself will be hugely rewarding and worth every effort.

In future chapters, I will advise you how to go about the dumping, which is a multifaceted procedure. When you have read these chapters you will experience a supremely uplifting sensation of release from inner complication and baggage. You will find yourself free at last to allow easy flowing lines of communication between your mind, body and spirit. Real progress will be there for all to see just as soon as you start to make the little changes, one after another, that are suggested in the chapters to come. You will have commenced the process of reconnecting your disconnected self and, as a direct and predictable consequence of your actions, depression will lift.

31

Thought-stopping strategies

Life does not consist mainly – or even largely – of facts and happenings. It consists mainly of the storm of thoughts that are forever blowing through one's mind.

Mark Twain (1835–1910)

We are about to discover, in this short chapter, how to begin to stop, at will, the storm of thoughts that are forever blowing through our minds. This will allow us to interrupt, minimise and eventually eliminate, all those anxiety-producing, depressing and self-defeating thoughts which plague us so much of the time.

The procedures for doing this are enjoyable and straightforward. We shall call the process 'SOS' because this is an internationally recognised distress code that you are unlikely to forget and it just happens to be an abbreviation for the experiences I want you to enjoy: silence, oblivion and serenity.

To achieve a high measure of success in SOS, you will need to set aside ten minutes a day for thirty consecutive days to practise immersing your mind into this tranquil but, at the same time, disciplined state, which is not unlike yoga. The dividends you will get for this small investment in time are immeasurable. Your recovery will be greatly accelerated and you will continue to enjoy the therapeutic benefits of SOS for the rest of your life.

Press on with your practice sessions, even if you are one of those people (like me) who find new techniques a little tricky to understand at the outset. This is like escaping to an internal paradise for a few enchanted moments and discovering, on your return, that a curative lotion has been applied to your troubled mind. It is too good to give up just because you may not be able to get it right the first few times you try.

The type of thoughts we are going to target and stop are the unwanted, repetitive, sometimes irrational and frequently obsessive ones that invade our minds when we should be considering more important matters, or enjoying our leisure time.

The things you will need to prepare for your first SOS experience, which, ideally, should commence today or tomorrow, are: a lighted candle, a quiet, darkened room or a safe, peaceful hideaway, and the freedom of mind that comes with knowing that you will not be disturbed by anyone, or anything, during your ten-minute session. No ticking clocks, mobile phones, or other potential distractions.

The object of the first session is to empty your mind for one beautiful moment of all thoughts, to stop thinking, to experience nothingness. If this sounds too easy, just wait until you try! To begin with, it might seem almost impossible to silence all those irritating little thoughts for a mere two seconds, let alone ten or twenty, but with persistence and regular sessions of SOS you will succeed in emptying your mind for several minutes at a time. By then, you will be primed for the first of many bonuses to come in future chapters: you will be ready to absorb techniques that will allow you to use more of your mind than usual; you will be in a position to empower yourself to beat depression.

In order to get started, place the lighted candle on a table or on a stable surface in front of where you are going to sit, make yourself comfortable, close your eyes and concentrate on the flickering of the flame in the darkness. For as long as possible, think of nothing; do not entertain any thoughts of any kind in your mind at all. If a thought enters your head, blink, flick it out, and start again.

Ten minutes of SOS a day, for thirty days, that's all I ask. You have no idea how much benefit you stand to gain from this part of the exercise, and the multiple gains to come when we are in a position to put together all the pieces of the puzzle.

32

Using your mind to beat depression

Let us train our minds to desire what the situation demands.
Seneca (4 BC–AD 65)

Master this concept and life gets easier.

The situation demands that we train our minds to beat depression and that is what we shall do. In this part of the book we are going to train our minds to neutralise anger, tame fear, get active, sleep well, practise positive imagery, increase self-esteem and learn to forgive.

To make solid progress in the remaining seven chapters of this section, I must ask you to participate in the mind exercises and other mini-assignments I shall give you, regardless of any initial misgivings or scepticism you may have. Put all doubts on hold for a while, defer judgement, at least until you reach the end of Part Four.

The tool we are going to use to derive maximum benefit from the challenges ahead is revised thinking, a subject that we touched on in Chapter Two. Thoughts are all-powerful and it is our own thoughts that play a major role in making us depressed (or otherwise) and in keeping us depressed. All the spectacular creations of humanity (such as the Eiffel Tower or the *Mona Lisa*) and the less spectacular ones (such as the Milton Keynes Shopping Centre or the Millennium Dome) began as mere thoughts. From the thought came the idea, from the idea came the plan, and from the plan the real thing evolved.

Your feelings of depression first came into being as thought. This book started as one, simple thought. I liked the idea and took it forward. If my second thought had been 'No, I can't/won't do it', you wouldn't be reading this now. Likewise, if you allow yourself to think, 'I can't' or 'I won't participate in these silly mind exercises', you slam the door on recovery.

Understandably, when we are depressed, we can make the mistake of assuming that our feelings are at fault, when the real problem is probably the way we are thinking about life in general. Many of us have a tendency to blame ourselves for everyday events that happen and to put the worst possible interpretation on things that are said to us.

This misguided and rather selective way of thinking is self-defeating and further fuels our feelings of low self-esteem and depression. To recover from depression quickly and to overcome all obstacles in the path of your recovery, you will need to adopt a new way of thinking, as briefly outlined in Chapter Two, namely one which is forward-looking and blame-free. In the following chapters you will learn how to differentiate between outmoded thinking and revised thinking.

Approach these chapters with an open mind and a willingness to experiment with the exercises and ideas suggested and very soon you could be amazed at your progress. If you haven't already scheduled time for your first session of SOS (silence, oblivion and serenity) as suggested in the previous chapter, do it now. It is an important preparatory step in preparing your mind for what you are about to accomplish.

33

Neutralising anger

A soft answer turneth away wrath:
but grievous words stir up anger.

The Bible, Proverbs 15:1

When you are angry – use one of these five routines.

Anger is a logical reaction to many real-life situations and confirmation that we are responding in an alert manner to an undesirable state of affairs. However, the way in which we handle our anger in response to provocation, frustration or bad news determines whether the outcome will be the best available in the circumstances, or potentially depression-inducing.

Before we learn how to neutralise our own anger, let's first observe how some people mismanage their anger and succeed primarily in damaging themselves: listen to people arguing, and you will hear the determination of each party to hold on to their 'little bit of truth', to defend it as if their life depended on it. Such limiting assumptions carry a heavy price in terms of pain, conflict and anxiety. Convincing yourself that you must be right (in contrast to other people deciding you are right) is the great booby prize in life, the one unhappy people settle for.

At one time or another, most of us find ourselves involved in situations which can give rise to anger. Sometimes, however, it is unwise, irrational or inappropriate to express those feelings directly. For instance, many of us have found ourselves in circumstances where we've known that expressing our anger will get us nowhere.

This may happen even when we are careful to express ourselves in a reasonable and non-threatening manner, but it usually happens when we have been insensitive to somebody else's feelings, at a difficult time of the month, or after one drink too many.

We are all angry people – some of us just show it more than others. Anger is usually triggered by an event, an unkind remark, a person's behaviour towards us or our interpretation of any one of those things. It sets off our stress hormones, adrenalin, noradrenalin and cortisol, arousing tension in the body.

Holding on to anger is dangerous to health. Suppressed or internalised anger can lead to high blood pressure and can make depression even worse. If something or someone has made you angry, or if you have made someone else angry and you regret your actions, rectify the situation with the person concerned at the earliest opportunity, offering a sincere apology, if appropriate.

If it is just not practical or possible to do this, release those feelings of anger and frustration in the privacy of your home, or some other safe haven. Suggestions to help you accomplish this are included in the following five exercises.

Act out your anger

Once you are alone at home, or somewhere that you consider to be a safe environment, put on some lively music, turn up the volume, and immerse yourself in the sound and the beat of the music. Allow yourself to work out and release your feelings of anger and frustration by dancing and singing along with the music, cursing, swearing, jumping, shouting or screaming at will, until you have exhausted and purged yourself of all harmful energies.

Breathe and believe in the power of words

Turn off the radio, TV and any music that may be on, sit down, take off your shoes, relax and take three slow, deep breaths, and say the words, 'I am becoming calm, I am becoming more and more calm, I am calm', until it is true. Now link the source of your anger with the culprit in a dismissive and non-confrontational manner. For instance, if you work in a pub, restaurant or shop and a regular customer has angered you, tell yourself something like, 'This guy is a real pain, but we need his money and I love this job. He means nothing to me personally and I refuse to give him another thought', or 'Now that I am relaxed and calm, I will work out a strategy so that this won't happen again.'

The letter from hell!

Now it's your turn to have some fun and derive some real benefit from your anger at the expense of the perpetrator of your emotional turmoil. While it can be tremendously therapeutic to act out your anger as suggested in the first example, or to stare it out as in our next exercise, the person who most needs to hear and understand your pain is you. Letting the offender have it in the form of a 'no holds barred' letter can release your anger and make emotional resolution easier to achieve. Allow yourself the freedom of writing a letter of protest and pour out all your pent-up emotions and negative feelings on to the page. Spare the offender nothing. Do not censor your letter in any way. Be careful! Do not mail this letter. It is exclusively for your therapeutic benefit. When you have finished it, destroy it.

The healing mirror

Another way to deal with anger is to confront it head on in the mirror. Don't be tempted to shy away from your image just because your angry self looks so distressed. Hold your nerve and continue to look. You will very quickly feel the urge to calm down if only because you look ridiculous when fuming and angry. At this point in the exercise you may find tears welling up in your eyes. That's good. Very good. Already venom and anger are bailing out through the windows!

Imagination to the rescue

This final suggestion is my personal favourite. When you have wronged someone and tried your level best to put things right, but the person concerned just won't accept your apology, or when you believe you have been wronged, but know you haven't a cat in hell's chance of being offered an apology, use your imagination. Imagine that your apology has now been accepted on the understanding that you learn from this episode and do not repeat your mistake. Likewise, if you are due an apology which is never likely to be forthcoming, imagine you have received and accepted it.

Without saying anything further on the matter to the person concerned, treat him or her as if all is forgiven and neither of you have any further grievance. This simple adjustment in your head relieves you of all further responsibility in the matter. It also helps to relieve anger, guilt (if you have any) and pain. You feel better and the other party cannot believe that you can be so reasonable.

34

Taming fear

There is no terror in a bang, only in the anticipation of it.

Alfred Hitchcock (1899–1980)

When you feel the fear, tame it with the 'mind game'.

Taming fear! This sounds *scary*. Admittedly, it's not the easiest of things to do, but, since you've made it this far, I think you will find the challenges ahead to be more manageable than you might suppose. Later, towards the end of the chapter, we are going to have some fun at the expense of someone who once put the fear of God into you. After that, you will be in a position to gauge just how much progress you are already making. Even before we get into therapy in Part Five.

If we gathered up all the fearful thoughts that exist in the mind of the average person and looked at them objectively, we would see that the vast majority of them are useless.

Fearful thoughts take many different forms: we become afraid of situations in which we might make a fool of ourselves in front of other people or in which we might fail to live up to our personal expectations or the expectations of other people; we avoid certain people, situations and activities; we enter into a predictable rut and then become afraid because we know we have let ourselves down again. This cycle of self-destructive energy – from ourselves to ourselves – can have devastating consequences; it has the effect of bringing to fruition the self-fulfilling prophecy: you become so afraid of losing control that you do lose control.

In order to face down fear, we need to face the 'deathbed' test. You can do this right now by asking yourself, what are my worst fears? Then, simply ask yourself, will I fear these things on my deathbed? Our immediate answer is to say yes. But if we think about it, we may find that the thing (or things) we fear most today, we would not even remember at the end of our lives.

Now that we have established that in all probability you wouldn't give these fears the time of day in the fading twilight of your life, let's get into the routine of taming fear in everyday life. Here are some guidelines to help you in times of despair:

Confronting fear

An effective way of taming fear before it has a chance to creep up on you and get a grip is to develop your own plan for what to do when fear threatens. In order for you to achieve this, it will be helpful for you to sketch out two plans:

Plan A reminds you that you still have the option to go on making yourself miserable and depressed by rolling over and letting your fears terrorise and torture you as you did in your days of outmoded thinking. The idea behind this plan is to make you aware of how you will feel if you decide to do nothing, if you decide by default.

Plan B is just the opposite. This plan shows you how you can take precautions so that you do not become frozen with fear when confronted by a difficult situation or someone who used to frighten you. This plan brings your new powers of revised thinking into play and you refuse to dwell on matters that might otherwise depress and defeat you.

In this plan, for instance, whenever fearful thoughts try to invade your mind, you may decide to switch your thoughts to a happy occasion, one that gave you much pleasure. When confronted with someone you find difficult to deal with, you may decide to make use of the following routine.

Taming fear through comedy

With this simple technique, you can teach fear a thing or two about the overwhelming power of comedy. This mind game is a defensive strategy to be deployed when someone else is directing anger or abuse at you and you might otherwise have become fearful or in danger of losing your temper. Be careful! Do not laugh at the angry person during this routine.

1. Imagine that the angry or abusive person standing before you is either stark naked, or dressed only in their underclothes.
2. As the person's voice begins to rise, and the anger or abuse escalates, try to imagine how ridiculous he or she would sound if music were accompanying this verbal onslaught.
3. Try to imagine what sort of childhood and upbringing this naked or near-naked specimen must have suffered to end up an adult like this.
4. Congratulate yourself for remaining calm and in control. You're the winner!

Avoiding the panic button

In the process of learning new and unfamiliar survival skills and at the same time recovering from depression, there are bound to be setbacks, times when you don't get things quite right and it all goes momentarily pear-shaped. *Don't press the panic button* and give up on these proven techniques – they will work for you if only you give yourself a chance to win.

Imagine that you are a reasonably competent cook and you have just had one of the very latest and most sophisticated ovens delivered to your home. Would you really expect to produce your finest roast on the first attempt? Of course not, but perhaps you would after a little experimentation and a few setbacks along the way. These state-of-the-art life skills you are learning now take a little getting used to as well – just don't give up!

> *I have often been afraid, but I would not give in to it. I simply acted as though I was not afraid, and presently the fear disappeared.*
>
> Theodore Roosevelt, twenty-sixth President of the United States (1858–1919)

35

Getting active

Action is consolatory. It is the enemy of thought and the friend of flattering illusions.

Joseph Conrad (1857–1924),
Nostromo

Physical exercise – a little a day helps to keep depression at bay.

One of the most obvious signs of depression is that we become less active. Everything seems to be such a chore and since we get little or no satisfaction from what we do, we tend to do nothing, allowing ourselves to become stagnant. Many years ago, when I was depressed, I remember spending more time thinking about life, than living it.

When we are on a downward spiral, there is a tendency to think about everything first, then to deliberate on our deliberations, then concern ourselves with the problems of our deliberations until, in effect, we are too exhausted from all this thinking to do anything at all, and so we don't. Action becomes out of the question.

There is a well-documented heaviness to depression – lethargy in the extreme – a disabling sluggishness that sucks and flattens our normal 'get up and go'. We can feel helpless and alone as if we have been transported to a planet with ten times the gravitational pull of earth. It is this overwhelming heaviness that makes the mere thought of exercise less than delightful for many, and a real challenge for some.

It would greatly help your recovery if I could tempt you into a little gentle exercise. The key to success is to do a little bit every day, starting today.

Unless there are any medical reasons why you should not exercise, such as heart trouble, high blood pressure, unexplained pains in the chest, dizziness, fainting, or a bone or joint problem that could be made worse by exercise, I am going to ask you to give your recovery a major boost by putting down the book for a few moments at the end of the next paragraph and getting active.

Without any further thought or deliberation, I would like you to do one or more of the following: do some gentle stretching exercises on or in your bed, take a brisk walk or run on the spot until you become just a little breathless. Alternatively, a few press-ups, perhaps, or whatever you can safely and comfortably manage in the way of exercise. Please accede to my request now, before continuing with the chapter, unless there is a medical or overriding reason why you should not.

After an active break

Are you a little breathless? If so, well done. The hardest part of any programme for getting fit and active is the first part – getting started – the bit you have already completed! From now on, things are going to get easier and you are going to feel better for taking some daily exercise. Nothing too daunting, just a little a day to keep depression at bay. If you were not ready or able to take some exercise (I know, some days it can feel impossible to do what must be done) why not try again tomorrow? You can easily catch up and you will at least begin to sample a feeling of wellbeing.

Exercise has proved to be effective in:

- Clearing our minds and enhancing levels of concentration.
- Reducing insomnia.
- Improving muscle tone.
- Rejuvenating our immune systems.
- Improving digestion.
- Stimulating blood flow and vascular circulation.
- Regenerating skeletal joints.
- Building up stamina and reducing fatigue.
- Decreasing cholesterol levels.
- Lowering blood pressure.
- Strengthening our heart and lungs.
- Cleansing our mental, physical, and emotional systems.
- Strengthening our respiratory system.
- Preventing coronary heart disease.
- Burning calories and helping to keep our bodies in good shape.
- BEATING DEPRESSION.

When we do something that requires an element of physical exercise, we awaken a part of ourselves that otherwise lies dormant. The problem, when we are depressed, is getting started in the first place. If this is your problem, an effective way to overcome inertia is to make a deal with yourself that you will do something for ten minutes only, before deciding if it is really as undesirable as you feared. If it is, you can then give yourself permission to quit. What often happens, I find, is that after ten minutes the inertia is overcome and one's on one's merry way.

36

Quality sleep

God bless the inventor of sleep, the cloak that covers all men's thoughts, the food that cures all hunger . . . the balancing weight that levels the shepherd with the king.

Miguel Cervantes (1547–1616),
Don Quixote

The most wonderful thing about quality sleep is the joy of waking up refreshed and restored and feeling energetic, alert and full of life. Sadly, this is seldom the experience of the depressed person, who is more likely to snatch intermittent patches of sleep between periods of anxiety and feel exhausted and lifeless upon awakening.

One of the most infuriating and frustrating problems in life is the inability to fall asleep when we retire for that purpose. Although most of us can tolerate the occasional night of sleepless torture, insomnia that stems from anxiety or depression tends to repeat itself on a regular basis. The more you can't sleep, the more anxious you become each night because you feel you won't be able to fall asleep easily and, sure enough, it becomes a self-fulfilling prophecy. The next night, there you are again – frustrated, wide awake and even more debilitated than you were before.

A good night's sleep (or adequate rest at some other time if you are a shift worker) is essential to combat depression and to keep us healthy. We sleep in different ways at different times of the night. One of the most important types of sleep is called Rapid Eye Movement (REM) sleep. It comes and goes throughout the night and takes up about 20 per cent of our overall sleeping time. During REM sleep our brain is active and our eyes move quickly from side to side as we dream.

The rest of the time, during non-REM sleep, the brain is less active and hormones are released into the bloodstream to facilitate essential self-maintenance and repair work throughout our bodies. Physical changes are taking place at the same time. For instance, blood pressure drops and our breathing and heartbeat slow down.

Lack of sleep adversely affects our overall mental and physical health: our heart, brain and digestive system all suffer as a direct result of sleep deprivation.

When we enjoy quality sleep, we are largely unconscious or unresponsive: we lose sensation along with our short-term memory and the ability to think properly. Sleep comes of its own accord, it does not occur in response to anything specific that happens to us but it can, nonetheless, be induced by a relaxed frame of mind. This, of course, is the problem: how do you achieve a relaxed frame of mind?

Some people find that listening to soothing music is effective; some find a hot bath helps; others prepare themselves for a good night's rest by making love to their partner or taking the dog for a walk. For me, a cup of hot chocolate is the answer. Avoid drinking a lot of alcohol: it may help you to fall asleep but you are far more likely to wake up in the night.

If something is troubling you and there is nothing you can do about it before retiring to bed, make a note of the problem on a piece of paper with a view to dealing with the matter tomorrow. No longer do you have a cloud of anxiety hovering over your pillow, you have an entry on a piece of paper instead. Now you can relax, and dream peacefully.

37

Positive imagery

Whether you believe you can or can't, you're right.

Henry Ford (1863–1947)

This powerful mental exercise is uplifting and enjoyable.

Positive imagery is about visualising precisely what you want from life. How can you be certain that you will get what you visualised? My experience could be useful. In the 1980s my life was going nowhere. I had so many problems and, seemingly, no hope of any solutions to them. Then, in desperation, I turned to positive imagery, which is a specific form of visualisation – knowing what you want in life and seeing yourself in that role until it really happens. Within one year I had solved all of my problems and my life was back on track and going in a worthwhile direction, the direction I had visualised.

Although some of my closest friends and my financial adviser had warned me that my intentions were not viable, I allowed myself to do what I really wanted to do, which was to study stress management and, when qualified, to set up in practice as a consultant. Within a few short years, I was chairman and chief executive of the UK's largest stress management group with ninety-two franchised consultancies.

Again, in 1995 – the year that I experienced two devastating strokes and lost everything including my health, my house and my business – it was positive imagery that I used to get back my life. As I stared up at the ceiling from my hospital bed, partly paralysed on one side of my body and unable to speak properly or comprehend the meaning of words, I visualised myself fit and well and writing a book. Five years on, I am 100 per cent fit and my book *After Stroke* was published by Thorsons here in the UK and in America in 2000. At the time of writing this, it's having its third print run.

Enough about me, let's consider your best way forward, but first a little explanation and theory is called for.

Your conscious mind works rather like a spotlight of awareness, highlighting some areas of your immediate existence, while ignoring others. What you pay attention to and how you respond is determined largely by what matters most to you in a given situation. If you know what you want in life and imprint that vision time and time again on your mind through positive imagery, that spotlight of awareness will become trained and tuned to highlight aspects of life that will enable you to get what you want. Similarly, if you think only about how depressed you are, that same spotlight of awareness will focus on every possible reason and piece of evidence to confirm depression.

Give some thought in the next few days to what it is that will make your life meaningful and fulfilled. Don't just say, 'lots of money' or 'winning the lottery', because all the money in the world will not necessarily make your life meaningful or fulfilled. There are more than enough depressed and suicidal millionaires in the world to ram that point home.

If you single-mindedly want to do something particular in life, see yourself in your mind's eye already doing it. Visualise yourself doing whatever it is that you have an overwhelming desire to do or to achieve. Supercharge your emotions with thoughts and images of what it is you are going to do. Should you be one of the many millions of people in the world who cannot visually summon up mental pictures in their mind, don't worry – thinking about your dreams and intentions with real passion and enthusiasm will get you precisely the same result. Positive imagery is simply a technique to lend reinforcement to the thinking process.

When would be the ideal time for you to practise positive imagery? Directly after your daily SOS session, when your mind is relaxed and crystal clear, would be a great time to start. Later, in Part Six, we will move on to your particular purpose in life.

38

Greater self-esteem

There's only one corner of the universe you can be certain of improving, and that's your own self.

Aldous Huxley (1894–1963),
Time Must Have a Stop

Self-esteem starts right here, right now.

Most people assume that self-esteem is a God-given gift, but it is not – it is a quality which can be learned and that is exactly what you're going to do now. Very few people feel completely happy with themselves all the time and this is no bad thing because we all have a tendency to make mistakes and say things we don't mean from time to time. If we had too high an opinion of ourselves we would not be able to accept when we are wrong and adapt or apologise accordingly.

If, however, you are lacking in self-esteem, if you have little pride in your own ideas or abilities, you effectively cut yourself off from experimenting with new ideas and getting to know interesting people. It is obvious to others from your body language, even before you open your mouth, that you have little regard for yourself. How can we change this unflattering self-image? We can start by beginning to have some respect for ourselves and by taming that arch-enemy of self-esteem – doubt!

In your dreams you are able to do some remarkable things. You can be in two different places at the same time, walk through walls, get along with all of your friends and associates and have passionate affairs with whomsoever you please. You can do all these things and more in your dreams because you don't doubt yourself.

In our waking state, most of us spend a tremendous amount of time and energy doubting ourselves. We question our self-worth and our capacity to do what needs to be done. We doubt our ability to overcome rejection, to make new friends and to win the heart of the person we want. We are using doubt in its most damaging and negative form to beat ourselves up. Of course, it makes sense to have a healthy respect for the positive side of doubt – avoiding harebrained decisions and actions – but if we can learn to eliminate the downside of doubt and start trusting in our natural abilities, we become a new person, one to whom others are attracted.

When you get right down to it, people with high self-esteem are men and women who are comfortable and at peace with themselves. They are genuinely happy with the way their lives are progressing, regardless of whether they are serving drinks or writing bestsellers. They appear to have a strong presence because they are completely absorbed in the moment. In conversation with such people, you get the impression they are interested in you as a fellow human being. His or her mind isn't drifting elsewhere; all their energy, enthusiasm and interest is focused right there on you. Notice how they have a tendency to say pleasing, complimentary things that court popularity. They will ask about *you* because they know that your world revolves around you and, like the rest of us, you love to be flattered.

After many years in stress management consultancy, helping people to embrace and overcome problems in their lives in order to beat depression, it is clear to me that the easiest way to feel good about yourself is to make someone else feel good. Do something good for someone else once in a while without seeking reward or recognition. I have learned the truth in the saying: 'what goes around, comes around'. Whether it's taking the trouble to congratulate someone for a job well done, offering support and encouragement, a friendly phone call, an unexpected favour or something more substantial, you will feel good and, over time, your self-esteem will become greater.

What I am about to ask you to do now and every time you are alone in the bathroom for the next thirty days, may strike you as downright ludicrous, but I want you to do it anyway. Why? Because it works! Stand tall and proud in front of the bathroom mirror and say the following words with authority, sincerity and conviction.

> 'I am a good person. I value myself.'

Many people hold themselves in low self-esteem and become depressed because they have few friends. If this sounds like you, you will need to implement two changes in order to make a favourable impact on your present circumstances: one affecting your basic thought processes, the other concerning your social behaviour. The latter is simplicity itself and will be great fun, and the former may well prove to be easier than you think because by the time you have completed this book and the integral exercises along the way, you will already have achieved the changes necessary for success, which include:

1. A subtle but important change in the way you think about other people so that you genuinely believe (as opposed to *think you believe*) that you want to get to know them.

2. Actually getting out there with the intention of *meeting* more people (instead of *seeing* and *ignoring* them). Most people are not psychic. If you want something, you are much more likely to get it if you ask for it. Call someone you know, or visit them, to make a date for coffee, shopping, a drink, a visit to the library or gym, etc. It could become a regular thing. There's safety and comfort and increased possibilities in numbers! As you progress further through this book, your self-confidence and your self-esteem are both destined to improve, so there is no need to dismiss this suggestion out of hand.

   If you don't know anyone, telephone a few of your favourite charities and offer a few hours of your time each week for free, perhaps as a street-collector. The chances are you will meet some very kind and warm-hearted people and, in time, it follows that you may be invited to some social get-togethers.

Here are some useful guidelines

- *Don't* be stand-offish. If you sit with your arms and legs crossed, or tightly clutching a glass, bag or plate, your body language shows that you feel uncomfortable and closed to communication, giving a clear message to others to 'keep away'.
- *Do* sit or stand where others can see you. When talking make frequent eye contact and occasionally gesture with your hands in a relaxed way (with your wrists and palms open and upwards, rather than clenched into fists).
- *Do* introduce yourself to others, rather than wait to be introduced – even if you are feeling nervous. You may be looking into the eyes of someone who would love to make you feel at ease.
- *Do* smile. The action of smiling, even if it's not sincere at the outset, actually lifts your mood and gives out a powerful and highly appealing body-language message: *I like being me – and maybe I am going to like you too!*

39

The ultimate challenge: forgiveness

And forgive us our trespasses, as we forgive them that trespass against us.

The Lord's Prayer, from the *Book of Common Prayer*

Crucial to your recovery – *forgive yourself* as well!

Forgiving is by far the most difficult undertaking I shall ask you to attempt in this book. I know, from my own life experiences, past and very recent, the exercises towards the end of the chapter will test you. Nevertheless, if you really are to recover from depression, if you are to go on to enjoy a happy, meaningful life, I cannot spare you now: you are too tantalisingly close to achieving a monumental step forward in life. Second only to the ability to love, forgiveness is the greatest test of our qualities as human beings.

The only way to heal the pain that will not heal itself is to forgive the person who hurt you. Not forgetting to forgive yourself at the same time for any complicity, omission, or personal responsibility in the matter. Forgiving erases the intensity of the hurt from your memory and allows you to move on. When you release the wrong-doer from the wrong, it's as if you are cutting a malignant tumour out of your inner self. You set a prisoner free, but you discover the real prisoner was you.

In demonstrating that forgiveness can positively enhance emotional health, Professor Carl Thoresen of Stanford University in the States, lead researcher for the Stanford Forgiveness Project, has said, 'Very few people understand what forgiveness is and how it works.'

What is forgiveness?

Forgiveness is the act of cancelling an emotional debt from the wrongdoer to you, and from you to yourself. It involves a conscious and deliberate process of revised thinking to bring about this total transformation of feelings from bitterness and resentment (or even hate) to feelings of genuine compassion. These humanitarian emotions allow your heart to open up and become receptive to the extraordinary act of will and courage necessary to complete the forgiveness exercises later in this chapter.

What if I am not yet ready to forgive?

If you are still reading, then clearly you have reached the stage whereby you are at least *prepared to contemplate forgiveness* even if you are not ready or able to forgive just yet. Already you have come a very long way along the path towards forgiveness. I cannot believe that you will persist in torturing yourself for ever now that relief from all that pain is almost within your grasp. Forgiveness is something that you can prepare to do despite your misgivings. Forgiving is a process that has a very definite start to it and you may be closer to the starting line than you thought possible days – even hours – ago. The start is deciding that in the end you will forgive, you will recover; you will have a better quality of life.

Why is reconciliation so hard after conflict?

Depressed people have particular difficulty in achieving reconciliation after experiencing hostility – whether it occurred either a week or more than fifty years ago. In the majority of instances, this is because as children we were never taught how to reconcile our differences with other people and now, as adults, we feel awkward about acquiring the skills to go about it.

Another reason so many people feel that they cannot contemplate reconciliation is their need to be proved right, to have the moral high ground, the dominant position. The person who reaches out to make peace is perceived as the one who has submitted. This, by implication, infers that he or she may have been the one in the wrong. This is sad, because the one who reaches out, the one who tries to heal the rift, regardless of right or wrong, is very likely to be the finer character.

It can be even harder to forgive someone who is dead. Or someone who isn't sorry for what they have done, or someone who is blissfully unaware of the hurt they have caused. Quite possibly, the offender did not deliberately set out to hurt you. Parents and children, lovers and sweethearts, husbands, wives, in-laws or ex's know a lot about this.

> Forgive yourself: life didn't come complete with a step-by-step instruction manual for getting it right every single time.

We are human, and this implies that we are going to make mistakes, mess up, lose our way, say things we regret and be downright selfish and unbearable once in a while. I am not a religious person myself, but I believe the most wonderful thing about saints is that they were human. Like us, they may have lost their tempers, got angry, scolded God, made mistakes and regretted them, but still they were awarded the 'Peace of God', which, to me, surpasses all understanding.

So, what is the big deal about getting things wrong from time to time? Why are we so hard on ourselves? Why cannot Mr, Mrs or Ms Perfect accept that life is a learning curve and that there is much to be gained from accepting our weaknesses and forgiving others and ourselves?

The core texts of the world's principal religions recognise that the quest for happiness is not without its challenges and obstacles. The experience of fulfilment would seem to involve some kind of spiritual journey through life, which at times appears almost to go beyond the limits of human emotion and understanding. Depression is a tragedy by any standards, but much good can come out of it if we are persuaded to address a matter which is long overdue: forgiving ourselves and others who have wronged us.

Doing it

There are three straightforward steps to forgiveness: Step 1 is dissolving resentment; Step 2 is identifying with the wrongdoer's possible motivation in a compassionate way; Step 3 is the act of forgiveness itself, which is forever irretrievable. You can't wake up tomorrow and decide to rescind it. Please note, the sequence and contents of these exercises are exactly the same regardless of whether you are forgiving yourself or other people.

Step 1: Dissolving resentment

Sit quietly, close your eyes and relax. Imagine yourself sitting alone in an empty, dimly lit theatre. You can sit in the front row, the back row, in a private box, or anywhere else you choose as long as you place the person or persons you are going to forgive on the stage. It could be someone from the past or the present, living or dead. It could be an image of yourself up there on the stage while you remain in your seat.

When, in your mind's eye, you see this person/these people, imagine wonderful things happening to them, the sort of things that would make them happy and contented without in any way threatening or saddening you. See their smiling face/s fill with delight and feel the warmth of their happiness touching you. Hold this image for a few moments, longer if you wish, before opening your eyes.

You can repeat this step daily, with a different person or group of people. Should you experience difficulty in visualising images in your mind, you can instead paint, draw on paper or create these scenes on your computer.

I want to, but . . . I just can't do it!

If you really can't overcome your resentment and find it in your heart to forgive, you must realise that it is your recovery that is at stake. If you cannot forgive the person who hurt you, you must dismiss him or her from your mind. See them as beneath contempt if that helps, and move on. Don't allow such a person to get in the way of your recovery.

Forgiveness is the only option in the end, but if your hurt has been so deep that you cannot deal with it without thinking of revenge, use the following technique:

Resentment workout: revenge

Skip this step if possible. Use only if necessary. Use only once. For some of us, even nice people, there is an unsavoury but necessary interim step to take before we can feel able to bring ourselves to forgive. Sometimes, a part of us needs to have revenge before we can move on. OK, let's get on with it.

Close your eyes, relax and think of all those people (or that one particular person) who are (is) hardest to forgive. What would you really like to do with them if you could have your way with each and every one of them? In your idea of a perfect world, what would you have them do to earn your forgiveness? Imagine it happening, play it through in your mind, enjoy it, savour it, and now get down to the details. Exactly how long do you want them to suffer for, and how much should they suffer? When you are satisfied you have worked through your resentment, that's the time to get down to the serious business of forgiving – yourself included.

Step 2: Understanding and identifying with the wrongdoer's possible motivation in a compassionate way

Try very hard to be compassionate in your thoughts of the other person. Bear in mind that they were probably trying to do the best they could with the limited resources and abundant problems they had at the time. Their priorities and values may be different from yours. Identify with the person's possible motivation and try to think of charitable reasons for the motivation behind what they did, or what they said, that hurt you so much. If you were responsible for contributing to the situation in some way, admit it, learn from your mistake, then release yourself and the other person from the situation once and for all.

Step 3: The act of forgiveness

Sit down, stand to attention or kneel, whichever seems appropriate to you. Close your eyes and say these words out loud, 'The person I need to forgive is . . . (name) and I forgive them for . . . (state succinctly what they did, or said, to hurt you).'

Repeat this three times, each time with increased emphasis, conviction, and absolution in your voice, and in your heart.

Well done. Now you can really concentrate on getting better and *you will succeed*.

Part Five

Therapy

40

Therapeutic thoughts

Our life is what our thoughts make it.

Marcus Aurelius (AD 121–180)

Treat yourself to the luxury of some nice thoughts!

Praise is the most wonderful tonic. It is not of paramount import-ance whether the uplifting message you receive is praise from someone you admire, from a complete stranger, or self-praise (congratulating yourself for refusing a chocolate, resisting the urge for yet another cigarette, or for motivating yourself to do the housework or to get up and take a walk). What matters is that the spotlight of your mind focuses on something good, something reassuring, and something nice about you, instead of languishing in the dark shadows of depression.

When we are depressed, we feel under-appreciated, as if no one, including ourselves, understands how hard we are trying to piece together the fragments of our lives and lift ourselves off this island of isolation. At times like this, it is important to stop what we are doing and give ourselves a pat on the back for a genuine achieve-ment, regardless of whether it is a great stride forward in our recovery, a minute but measurable step in the right direction, or a kind action for someone else.

Take a few moments to reflect on what you have been doing to improve your situation and don't forget to give yourself a huge helping of well-deserved praise for reading this book. This book may well be easy to read, but it's not easy to read and respond when you are depressed. You are doing that right now and I admire you greatly.

Take time out at the end of this chapter to congratulate yourself on your recent and past achievements and give some recognition to the special attributes you possess and the kind deeds you have done in your life. Think about what you have just read. Contemplate only the good things about you and your life for a while. Do this, and I believe you will begin to bring the hint of a smile to your lips and a lump to your throat. OK, so life has been mighty tough for a while now, but there are quite a number of things that are special and nice about you, aren't there?

Recognising our contribution ourselves can actually be more powerful and satisfying than hearing it from others, although, naturally, we love to hear those (rare) wonderful words of praise from loved ones, associates or the boss.

Sometimes, in the maelstrom of modern life, and particularly in the depths of depression, it is all too easy to forget about the worthy contributions we make to ourselves, our families, our friends and the people and businesses that we work for or did work for in the past, together with the donations we make to charities in terms of time or money.

Without doubt, each of us has something to commend ourselves for and many of us have so much for which to pat ourselves on the back that the occasion of finishing this chapter really ought to be a moment (or perhaps an evening) of celebration. A celebration of ourselves and the good things we have done, or tried to do.

41

Antidepressants

What other dungeon is so dark as one's own heart!
What jailer so inexorable as one's self!

Nathaniel Hawthorne (1804–64),
The House of the Seven Gables

Your doctor will know what is best for you.

Worldwide drug sales for antidepressants alone are predicted to reach $15 billion in the year 2002, according to the *Scrip Report* on depression and central nervous system disorders. This figure shows a staggering 100 per cent increase on the $7.1 billion spent five years ago, in 1997.

Sales of this magnitude stimulate massive investment in research and development and a new generation of antidepressant drugs is on its way. Benefits to consumers will include an improved range of Selective Serotonin Re-uptake Inhibitors (SSRIs) that will move on from Prozac and its successors, bringing improvements in mood without the side-effects of earlier antidepressants which can include dizziness, dry mouth and changes in behaviour.

Currently, there are many people who are reluctant to take medication of any kind to combat depression, especially mood-altering drugs. There are fears that antidepressants may prove addictive and, in some countries, the public have been frightened by reports of tranquilliser addiction and people have become wary of anything they perceive as having a similar effect. These reservations and fears need to be taken seriously but the current generation of antidepressants are less likely to lead to addiction or dependency.

The majority of people with depression gain relief with the original drug prescribed, but in the unlikely event that you experience unacceptable side-effects, you should tell your doctor, and an alternative drug may be suggested. Antidepressants are not all the same and in a minority of cases the only effective way to find the one that brings maximum relief with minimal side-effects is by trial and error.

I see no advantage in giving complex and potentially confusing information to readers about Tricyclics, Monoamine Oxidase Inhibitors (MAOIs), and Selective Serotonin Re-uptake Inhibitors (SSRIs), when the decision to prescribe or not to prescribe is the exclusive domain of physicians. However, Prozac warrants a mention because it has become the most popular antidepressant in the world. The manufacturers claim that patients typically show an improvement in their condition two to three weeks after being prescribed the drug. Unlike previous generations of antidepressants, Prozac has fewer undesirable side-effects although the drug is still controversial. The active ingredient in the drug is fluoxetine and

151

this inhibits the re-uptake of the brain chemical serotonin, boosting chemical levels in the brain and maintaining the brain in a higher state of arousal (not depressed).

Prozac has acquired a reputation for helping people overcome not only their basic symptoms of depression, but also a range of other problems that, until recently, were traditionally thought to require psychotherapy or counselling, such as lack of self-esteem, fear of rejection and extreme sensitivity to criticism. The drug is often prescribed for senior citizens with depressive symptoms because older people are considered to be able to tolerate the same starting dosage as younger patients, which is not the case for some drugs.

So much for getting on, how about getting off? Obviously, your doctor will advise you but here are the general principles: suddenly, as opposed to gradually, discontinuing any form of antidepressant treatment can have serious consequences for a very small minority of users and there is always a risk of some minor withdrawal symptoms. Choose the ideal time to gradually scale down your dosage as a preliminary to withdrawing from the drug altogether. A period when something exciting is happening in your life is the perfect time to quit. At the very least, ensure that things are moving your way and you have a definite and absorbing interest in life. In the unlikely event that you 'land heavily' and experience the flu-like symptoms caused by too-rapid cessation of the drug, all is not lost. You simply return to full dosage for a short period, and then, by arrangement with your doctor, you progressively scale down your dosage to zero over time.

42

The talking therapies

Conversation has a kind of charm about it, an insinuating and insidious something that elicits secrets from us just like love or liquor.

Seneca (4 BC–AD 65)

My experience in treating depressed clients either as individuals or as participants in my 'Beat Depression' initiatives and 'Tackling Under-Performance' workshops for companies has left me in no doubt that the talking therapies have an important part to play in beating depression, but now scientists have proved that depressed individuals can be livelier, happier and more productive after just six sessions of psychotherapy.

A total of twenty-eight seriously depressed patients aged between thirty and fifty-three were monitored with SPECT (Single Photon Emission Computed Tomography) brain scans to check blood flow during a study commissioned by the Royal College of Psychiatrists in the UK in 1999. Fifteen patients were then given a six-week course of antidepressants and the remaining thirteen were given six one-hour sessions of interpersonal psychotherapy. After six weeks all the participants' brains were scanned again.

Brain scans could show whether the patients felt better because when they talked about their troubles the blood flow increased through the part of the brain that is believed to be responsible for depression. The scans on the group of fifteen people undergoing treatment with antidepressants showed a marked increase in blood flow to specific areas of the brain during the trial period. The scans on the group of the thirteen receiving psychotherapy also showed a dramatic increase in blood flow to specific areas of the brain. The effect was similar to that achieved by antidepressants, but therapy also managed to affect a part of the brain untouched by drugs.

Those who had received psychotherapy also showed a marked increase in activity in the area of the brain thought to control body movements and co-ordination. Stephen Martin, a consultant psychiatrist at Cherry Knowle Hospital in Sunderland, said: 'This is the largest study ever done using brain scans in sequence to monitor depression. It's fantastic to see that we have got some areas of the mind switching on in sequence in the same way as with medical treatment. Certainly, talking works. The conclusion is that patients do best with a combination of structured therapy and antidepressants. I think the process of being listened to is important, but there is good evidence that interpersonal psychotherapy is a lot more effective than just talking. It's not a quick discussion – it is quite intensive work linking the patient's depressed mood with their problems and helping them with quite strong direction from the therapist.'

The patients involved in the study had all expressed symptoms of major depression at the outset, including sleep disturbance, weight loss or gain, fatigue and feeling unable to enjoy life. A survey six months after the study found that none of the patients had relapsed.

Every depressed person needs someone to talk to. Actually finding such a person, someone who really understands, is incredibly comforting and empowering. In those rare moments when we feel able to give voice to our confused and despairing thoughts, the greatest gift we can hope for is to have someone with the capacity to listen, who can gently and objectively help us make sense of our muddled ramblings, to show us – with especial sensitivity – the next step forward. I am convinced that this is why the talking therapies are so effective in helping people beat depression. Further information about 'Beat Depression' clubs or 'Tackling Under-Performance' workshops for companies can be obtained by writing to the address given in the 'Sources' section at the end of this book.

43

Music therapy

If music be the food of love, play on.

William Shakespeare (1564–1616),
Twelfth Night

Harness the power of music to comfort your soul.

Music possesses that special quality capable of making us uniquely aware of our innermost feelings. Somehow it becomes acceptable to shed tears while listening to a sad or moving song, the very same tears we struggle to suppress when confronted with our own or another's pain.

Music, as you will experience in the following exercise, can have an extraordinarily powerful effect in exploring and exposing the hidden motivations for our darkest moods and most private melancholy. It can function as a catalyst for discovering, soothing and disentangling deep-rooted sadness and internal mayhem.

Through music, we can recall the past, live the present and prepare for the future. Music has a wonderful – but sometimes daunting – ability to freeze images into recollections, releasing them later in life as images. As children, we dream of being adults. As adults, we dream of having our childhood again: the same childhood for some, a different one for others.

Music, as John M. Ortiz illustrates brilliantly in his book *The Tao of Music* (Newleaf, 1997) is a very powerful stimulus. Whenever music is associated with a particular moment, event or personal experience, the listener can attach very private imagery, feelings or personal meaning to that particular piece of music. Later, through music, one is capable of re-experiencing a mental and emotional representation of the essence of the moment when it was first heard. Sometimes, you play the music just to experience that moment once again.

In this short chapter you are about to learn how to harness the power of music to affect your own mood. If you ever wanted to be a record producer, this is your special moment. You are about to accomplish something far more important than producing a number one album, you are going to produce your own real-life music soundtrack that encapsulates special significance and meaning for you.

The result of your efforts will resonate deep within your subconscious mind and produce a therapeutic effect upon you. Your proposed music therapy tape will consist of a compilation of sounds that have hidden connotations for you. It will help you to connect and get in touch with your depressive mood and move on from it.

In order to proceed from this point you will need a cassette recorder and a blank tape for recording, or a rewriteable compact disc for your computer if it has sound recording facilities. If neither is available to you, ring a friend and ask to borrow their cassette recorder. Don't allow yourself to be deprived of this wonderful therapy. This is how you set about producing an effective music therapy tape or CD:

Get out your entire music collection! Don't hesitate just because you are feeling sceptical about the potential usefulness of this venture, just immerse yourself in choosing music that has distinctive memories for you and put them into three categories as follows:

Sad and lethargic
Choose several songs or pieces of music that best seem to capture your depressed state. Many depressed people find their choices for this category of music tend to be melancholic, slow-tempo numbers. Certainly, they should be tracks that have made a powerful impression on you in the past. If I were masterminding a compilation tape for myself, the Righteous Brothers' recording of 'You've Lost That Lovin' Feelin'' would come immediately to mind.

Moody, changeable, mid-tempo
Now choose a selection of songs or pieces of music that best seem to match your mood when you are neither particularly happy nor sad – just OK. Again, they should be tracks which hold a special meaning for you.

Upbeat, happy, *electrifying!*
For your final selection, pick recordings that take you back to your happy moments – the real high spots in your life. Many people find these are often tracks with a fast, vibrating tempo, music that is alive and bursting with passion and enthusiasm.

Take as much time as you need over your selections. For some, this assignment will be a rather enjoyable, whole-day occupation. When you feel you are ready, place your selections in order of extremes of mood from melancholy at the beginning to happy at the end (which, coincidentally, is how you would *like* to feel) and record your tape or CD in that order.

Play your homemade tape or CD several times a week for a few weeks and experience for yourself what music therapy can do for you. Over time, you may find your predominant mood moving distinctly away from the sad and miserable low point of depression you have been experiencing of late, hovering for a while in a more comfortable 'changeable to OK' frame of mind, before lingering for longer, *much longer*, in the happier emotions of life.

44

Dance therapy

Dancing, I believe, like virtue, must be its own reward.

Jane Austen (1775–1817),
Emma

Dance is a tonic for the heart as well as being highly beneficial to the body and spirit.

Dance is one of the oldest therapies known to man and yet it is only in recent years that dance has become an accepted therapeutic tool. Dance has the capability to lift dulled and depressed individuals out of their everyday tedium and to get their under-active bodies moving and stretching in time to the music. To a large extent it does away with the necessity for one to think or talk and it allows many alienated people to come together since dance can be a social outlet as well as a therapeutic tool.

One of the great joys of dance therapy is that it doesn't really matter whether you can do it properly or not. Lack of a convenient or willing dancing partner is of little significance either. I remember in the days when I was partly paralysed, fully depressed and striving to recover from the aftermath of my two strokes, I would put on some music and dance my way around the flat with the upright vacuum cleaner in an effort to get myself active and to make some impression on the household chores.

If you are by yourself, the ideal way to lighten your mood and get active is to select a piece of music with a good range of dynamics, something that starts slowly and builds up to a powerful crescendo. If necessary, move the furniture out of the way and allow your body, not conscious thought, to dictate your movements. There is no need to be self-conscious or to try to impress anyone, least of all yourself, just move to the music and let your hands and feet take over.

Dancing to your favourite choice of music is an excellent way to combat the blues, to defy depression, and to get the dusting done if you happen to have a duster in your hand at the same time. It can give real lift to your system even when you are feeling exhausted. Like exercise, once you get started, it triggers an exuberant rush through your body that can quickly jog you out of your black mood or distract your depressed train of thought.

Dancing is becoming ever more popular within many different age groups. If you can't dance too well but would like to go to a dance, don't worry about looking silly – the idea is to enjoy yourself with others, not to show off in front of them. If you think you would be too self-conscious to enjoy yourself, join a beginner's class where everyone will be at the same level and you can improve together, probably making some great new friends at the same time.

Whether you prefer dancing in nightclubs, discos or parties or prefer folk or ballroom dancing, you're getting really good exercise for your body and a fabulous lift for your spirit. Dancing is excellent for banishing the blues, improving stamina and increasing the strength of your legs. It can also help your joints remains supple and mobile and it's particularly good for your sense of balance – mind, as well as body!

Dance is not only an ideal way to get active, reduce tension and forget your troubles; it is a tonic for the heart as well as being highly beneficial to the body and spirit. It allows us to be moved by something other than depression and, if persisted in, can help to restore the soul and lighten the burden for those of us who are having a really hard time.

45

Pet therapy

Animals are such agreeable friends – they ask no questions, they pass no criticisms.

George Eliot (1819–80),
Scenes of Clerical Life

If you are depressed and alone, why not get a pet?

For some people, acquiring a pet can be the beginning of a magical partnership, and the act of ownership can mark the beginning of the end of depressive illness. In Great Britain alone, around seven million canine chums now share human homes and no fewer than eight million purring moggies are currently providing their owners with snug companionship.

Cats and dogs are more than just man's best friend. Recent studies have demonstrated that pets can help their owners in a variety of ways, including the lowering of blood pressure, improving mood and speeding recovery from depression and other illnesses. For example, heart attack patients who own pets are five times less likely to suffer a second heart attack within a year of the first, than patients who don't own pets.

Just having a pet around has been shown to reduce stress and improve the owner's general sense of wellbeing. In residential care homes, visits from animals have been shown to reduce depression and increase alertness in elderly people with dementia. People with physical disabilities can also benefit tremendously from having a pet. The sensuous and enjoyable act of running your hand over a dog's head, patting its side or tickling its tummy can be a different but rewarding physiotherapy exercise for those with limited arm movements.

Naturally, it is important for potential owners to realise that pets have feelings and needs as well. They have a moral right to be well cared for and looked after, to be kept healthy, fed and well nourished. Some potential owners, living in small flats in built-up areas and unable to get out much, might worry that, if they did get a pet, it might not be happy. Obviously, in the circumstances described, a little kitten, or a cat, would seem to be more practical than a dog.

It could be amusing to devise new ways to keep the little fellow entertained. With a kitten, encourage him to play with objects that he can investigate, such as a toy mouse. Provide cardboard boxes that he can climb into, cushions he can hide under, and possibly a cat climbing frame or activity centre. The pair of you will probably enjoy great fun, companionship and happiness together. Furthermore, the comfort and unconditional love provided by a warm, furry creature is often the precursor to being able to feel human tenderness again.

46

Massage

I like a man what takes his time.

Mae West (1892–1980)

Experience the power and importance of touch.

Massage has been shown to reduce blood pressure and alleviate some types of headache. It has been used effectively in the treatment of depression brought on by trauma. A study at the University of Miami Medical School has demonstrated that depressed patients who received the benefit of a half-hour massage had consistently lower levels of stress hormones during the massage and afterwards. Patients also reported they were able to sleep better.

One of the great joys of massage is that you are helpless on the couch with nothing to do. You have little choice but to lie back and let your therapist do with you as he or she wills. Massage releases tension, frees energy, removes physical blocks and feels good. It also brings awareness to the sensory nerves – just what you need when you are feeling depressed. Should you find yourself thinking or worrying about anything during your massage, simply abandon your thoughts and revert to the unparalleled luxury of lying there and being pampered in the name of therapy.

In the event that a commercial massage is beyond your budget, or if you would prefer to enjoy the benefits of massage alone at home, I strongly recommend you to treat yourself to the ecstasy of an Indian head massage dispensed with your own two hands. You don't need anyone else to help you to do this: you have the power to melt away pain and relieve stress in your own fingertips.

Narendra Mehta, who is totally blind, devised this and other massage techniques in India and brought them to the West. In his truly brilliant book *Indian Head Massage – Discover the Power of Touch* (Thorsons, 1999), he recommends the following self-administered method of head massage (please note that advice given in this chapter is not suitable for persons suffering from any chronic or acute health problems, such as whiplash injuries, migraine, epilepsy, psoriasis or eczema; if in doubt, please consult a doctor or professional therapist):

Relax; sit down comfortably in loosely fitting clothing with both feet on the ground and prepare to experience how a firm rub about the skull can relieve tension and how soothing strokes to the top of the head can give the sensation of lifting depression. Now follow these simple instructions:

- Gently massage the whole of the area of your scalp with thumbs and fingers, releasing any tension by friction and rubbing.
- Grasp fistfuls of hair at the roots and tug from side to side, keeping your knuckles very close to the scalp.
- Squeeze at the temples with the heels of the hands and makes slow, wide circular movements.
- Look down slightly and massage the back of the neck by squeezing and rolling the muscles. Start at the top of the neck and work your way down, first with one hand and then with the other hand. Repeat this a few times.

How do you feel now? Great, isn't it? Why not get into the habit of treating yourself to a head massage more often? You'll sleep more sweetly at night if you do.

47

Sex in depression

The follies that a man regrets most are those which he didn't commit when he had the opportunity.

Helen Rowland (1875–1950),
A Guide to Men

Most women know that sex is good for headaches.

Many people live happily without an active sex life, but for others, a satisfying sex life can be an important part of health and wellbeing. At the moment of climax, your brainwaves are being well and truly scrambled and this enjoyable sensation is not altogether different from the therapeutic benefits that can be derived from a less popular choice of therapy – ECT!

Setting yourself a desirable and attainable purpose in life, together with a realistic target date for its achievement, is therapeutic and may provide the additional benefit of helping you to banish depression from your life sooner rather than later. Chapters Fifty-six and Fifty-seven will give you an indication as to how you might set about achieving your goals, including this one. If you don't currently have a partner with whom to share an enjoyable sex life and you would like one, why not make yourself a binding commitment that within, say, one to twelve months from now, you will take the necessary steps to find the person of your dreams? In the meantime, let's discuss what sort of sexual problems can arise when you are depressed.

Two out of three people who suffer from depression lose interest in sex. It is important to understand that this lack of interest is only temporary and is as much a symptom of depression as feeling low, probably as a result of imbalances in brain chemistry. Reduced sexual activity may also be accompanied by weight loss/gain, reduced energy, and disturbed sleep. Other problems of a sexual nature that can occur as a result of depression are:

- Difficulty in becoming sexually aroused.
- Reduced sexual performance.
- Realising less pleasure than usual.
- Reduced energy levels.
- Difficulty in achieving or maintaining an erection.
- Premature ejaculation in men or not being able to ejaculate.
- Women may experience a loss of desire, vaginal dryness (which can make sexual intercourse painful) and difficulties in achieving orgasms.

Some antidepressants can cause sexual side-effects in around 40 per cent of patients. If you should experience such problems, your doctor is the person to talk to. Antidepressants from the latest generation of drugs are less likely to cause the type of sexual side-effects described above.

Remember, sexual problems are a symptom of depression. If you are missing the sex life you used to have and you would like to get it back, this is a sign of impending recovery and an incentive to beat depression by reading on and taking serious note of the advice in this book, before translating the advice into *action*.

48

Cognitive behavioural techniques

Whenever two people meet there are really six people present. There is each man as he sees himself, each man as the other person sees him, and each man as he really is.

William James (1842–1910)

A great many people think they are thinking when they are merely rearranging their prejudices.

'I think therefore I am,' wrote Descartes, the French philosopher and mathematician, in 1641. Our thoughts have a major effect on the way we perceive ourselves. At a basic level of consciousness, *we are our thoughts* and the content of those thoughts – whether positive or negative, loving or bitter, happy or depressed – has a direct impact on our emotions. Just one thought can have a profound effect on how we perceive the world.

To a greater or lesser extent, we act on the strength of our emotions. Because of this, the thoughts we have can influence the quality of our lives, our behaviour and our relationships with others.

In my view, based upon many years of counselling highly stressed and depressed clients, the most important factor in bringing about positive and highly beneficial changes in mood and behaviour, is exercising control over the birth of our own thoughts. The most powerful antidepressant drugs in the world cannot change an individual's underlying approach to life, but cognitive behavioural techniques of the type featured in this book can bring about lasting benefits.

This is possible because you can acquire an antidepressant skill you can use again and again without the need to rely on doctors and drugs. People who employ cognitive techniques find that their behavioural patterns change and they approach life more constructively; problems are more easily solved and life is more enjoyable.

Here are two real-life examples of cognitive behavioural therapy in action. The first case concerns Mary, a woman in her forties. You are not Mary, and your circumstances are not hers, but this case study will have served its purpose if you are moved to consider what it is that may be wrong, missing, undesirable or self-destructive in your own life.

Bear in mind that bitterness, betrayal, anger, loss, perceived failure and the desire for retribution and revenge – each of them classic ingredients for depression – can all show themselves in many different ways. The underlying root cause, the personal factors contributing to your own depressive illness, and the keys (actions necessary) for self-release, will, of course, be different to Mary's, but the possibilities for recovery can be just as good.

Mary's husband had been unfaithful at an office party. It had been a one-night stand, he had sworn never to do it again and she believed him. Yet, she could not forgive him: she was outraged by the betrayal. She had no desire to leave him – besides, they were Catholics and divorce was out of the question – but still she went on, day after day, night after night, punishing him, making herself more and more depressed.

I was disappointed at her lack of progress over a period of many weeks. She was making things worse for herself, not better. Her husband, having been forced by Mary to resign his previous job, had started a new one on the very day of the session I am going to tell you about, thus bringing to an end a dismal twelve-month period of unemployment. By her own admission, Mary had been difficult, nagging her husband incessantly, instead of treating this as an opportunity for a new beginning. Somehow, she had to be encouraged to think and act differently. I was in no doubt that subtlety was no longer an option.

'Mary, do you still love your husband?'

'Yes.'

'You do want this marriage to work?'

'I do.'

'Now this bit is not easy, but the time has come for you to forgive your husband.' I had no intention of breaking the silence that followed. She was going to respond, even if we went into extra time.

'I can't,' she admitted at last. 'I want to, I know I have to, *but I just can't do it!*'

'I have a simple technique for you, Mary, to make it possible, and I am going to give you the opportunity to practise it with some homework, and I require your word of honour, here and now, that you will complete it to the very best of your ability.'

'What is it that you want me to do?' I believe she was pleased I had acknowledged the fact that if she gave her word, she would keep it.

'Do I have your word? Without it we have nowhere to go.'

'Of course!'

'Have you got a clock on the mantelpiece at home, Mary?'

'Yes.'

'Can you see it from your favourite chair?'

'Yes.'

'Good. Now this is what I want you to do. Go home and relax. Look at the base of the clock and direct all of your resentment for your husband's betrayal towards that one spot. Concentrate like never before. Visualise yourself transferring every last drop of venom out of your heart and under the clock, secure in the knowledge that it will be there tomorrow, waiting for you, should you wish to retrieve it. Are you willing to give this a go, Mary?'

'Yes.'

'Next, I want you to prepare a special candlelit dinner with wine just for the two of you. Today is a cause for celebration for you both. Your husband has started his new job and you are about to take a great leap forward. Put on your most seductive dress and make love to him tonight. That is your homework, Mary. Same time next week?'

The next time Mary walked into my consulting room, I felt proud of her. She looked younger and even her complexion somehow seemed softer and smoother. There was sparkle in her eyes where before there had been only pain, mist and haziness. We didn't really need to say much. Life was going to get better and she and her husband were going to have peace of mind.

The details of this case are unimportant; the important thing is to distance yourself from the bitterness and resentment of the past and to think about the way forward.

The second example of cognitive behavioural therapy in action concerns myself, and we have already touched upon this in Chapter Thirty-seven, the chapter in which I introduced you to the potential benefits of positive imagery.

At the beginning of 1995, I was the chairman, chief executive and founder of a nationwide group of ninety-two franchised stress management consultancies, enjoying the fruits of my achievements: satisfaction, life in the fast lane and a rather grand lifestyle. By the end of the same year, I had virtually nothing, not even my health. Two major strokes in August had left me brain-damaged with the carotid artery to one side of my brain destroyed. I was partly paralysed on one side and unable to read, write or talk with any degree of normality.

On the plus side, my somewhat dry sense of humour had not deserted me and I knew a thing or two about stress management.

Using the same cognitive tools that I am teaching you, I succeeded in convincing myself that the only thing that mattered was getting well. Five years on, I have reclaimed both my health and my happiness and succeeded in winning the heart of the most wonderful woman in the world, to whom this book is dedicated. Those of you who are depressed as a result of stroke or serious illness will benefit from reading my previous book, *After Stroke*, which is a complete, step-by-step blueprint for getting better.

Are you ready for an assignment? When you turn the page, I am going to show you one of my favourite ways by which you can control your thoughts and lighten your mood. You, in return, are going to master this method because it will serve you well for the rest of your life.

Part Six

↑ Up You Come ↑

49

Hot baths and mind games

It is the height of luxury to sit in a hot bath
and read about little birds.

Alfred, Lord Tennyson (1809–92),
Said upon having hot water installed in his new house

Some people haven't taken a bath for years! In this high-tech, energy-efficient age, millions of people miss out on the therapeutic benefits of a hot, leisurely bath in preference to a quick shower. Edmund Wilson (1895–1972), the noted US critic, had this to say about my favourite early morning routine: 'I have had a good many more uplifting thoughts, creative and expansive visions while soaking in comfortable baths in well-equipped American bathrooms than I have ever had in any cathedral.'

The purpose of this chapter is to prepare you for an important exercise that we shall address in detail later. With this aim in mind, I must tempt you into the bathroom for a luxuriously long and uninterrupted hot bath, complete with a generous measure of a relaxing, aromatherapy bath essence.

The bath essence ideal for the mind games we are going to play is a blend of two essential oils: geranium and rosewood. In my view, the best value product on the UK market that meets these criteria comes from Boots, the chemists. It is their own brand and comes in a dark red bottle with a copper coloured cap and costs, at the time of writing, less than £3 for a 400ml bottle – and no, I don't have any financial interest in the company.

If you are traditionally more of a 'last thing at night' person in the hygiene department, I can assure you that this particular bath will do much more for your recovery and sense of wellbeing than an evening in front of the television or surfing the Internet.

It is essential for you to be able to relax comfortably in the bath for this session of self-therapy. If you don't have a headrest to lounge back on, place a couple of fluffy towels on the ridge of the bath for you to rest your head on. This is quality time we are looking for here, not a rapid scrub and an out-you-get quickie! You won't be in the mood to do what is required of you if the kids (grown-up or the tiny variety) can come barging in on you and please turn off any radio, TV or loud music that could disturb the session you are about to embark on.

Relax and enjoy the luxury of your hot bath with the mind-soothing aroma of geranium and rosewood. Without the need for a candle or a dimming of the lights, go into SOS mode for a few minutes as described in Chapter Thirty-one. When your mind is calm, allow your thoughts to wander to what it is that you would do with your life to make it meaningful if there were no restrictions whatsoever on your right to happiness. When you get out of the bath, note down your thoughts. We shall be referring to them later.

50

Friends

We have fewer friends than we imagine,
but more than we know.

Hugo von Hofmannsthal (1874–1929)

I'll get by with a little help from my friends.

This chapter is addressed mainly to friends and relatives of the depressed. As a rule, I start each chapter of my books with an appropriate quotation. This time I must open with two: the one we have just read, which is so poignant and relevant to those of us who are ill and depressed; and the quotation that follows by Anaïs Nin, the French-born American writer of novels and short stories (1903–77). On first reading her words, they can sound a bit grandiose, over-dramatic even, but over the years I have come to realise that these words are pertinent in every respect: *'Each friend represents a world in us, a world possibly not born until they arrive, and it is only by this meeting that a new world is born.'*

There is no doubt in my mind that my life has been enriched and broadened (and humbled at times) by the idiosyncrasies of my various friends. Quite apart from the thrill, excitement and pleasure of their company, there is the reassurance and contentment of simply being amongst friends that is an integral part of their tried and tested companionship. I have done many things (not all of which are to be recommended) that I would never have dreamed of doing if it were not for one or other of my friends.

In a perverse sort of way, I consider myself fortunate to have suffered a couple of strokes, not least because it was a telling opportunity to discover who my real friends were. Not surprisingly, after losing virtually everything including my health and my wealth, my fair-weather friends were nowhere to be seen, but my real friends (the ones who take me for who and what I am – the good, the bad and the outrageous!), they made it clear, in their own different ways, that they were there for me.

Do you know someone who is depressed? This could be your moment to do something helpful and compassionate for a friend, or a future friend, in need. Arrange to meet and encourage them to talk about their worries, their fears and about what they think might have caused their depression in the first place. The important thing here is to *listen*, to discuss possible solutions and sources of support, but to avoid telling them what to do or imposing a solution upon them. If they have not already been to see their doctor, encourage them to do so. You could offer to go with them. This can be tremendously supportive for depressed people who don't know which way to turn and lack the clarity of thought and momentum to do anything constructive to help themselves.

During the three- to four-year period that it took me to completely recover from my second stroke, I used to wonder why on earth some of my hard-working friends with busy lives of their own would travel hundreds of miles over a weekend to cheer me up, and then travel all the way back home again. At the time, this seemed to me to go way beyond the call of duty for even the closest friend, but there is no denying that their efforts provided a much-needed boost to my self-esteem, which had suffered a series of knock-backs.

Sadly, so many of us wait until we need something from someone before we take the trouble to get to know him or her. Not surprisingly, we are frequently disappointed because when we need something from someone and they know it, they are bound to be on their guard, defensive even, because for the sake of their own self-respect, if for no other reason, they have to be able to determine whether or not we are sincere.

Another observation that is guaranteed to terminate a potential friendship prematurely is jealousy. Let's be candid here. Have you ever found yourself secretly wishing that someone else would foul-up and fail? I know I have. If we are going to offer genuine and lasting friendship we must be prepared to delight in the success of others – even when that puts us in the shade once in a while. It's important to know that there is more than enough success to go round. If you have yet to taste your share of success, I have good news for you. You are working your way towards the chapters that can make all the difference to your future success and happiness. You are almost there.

Some special friends, usually older and wiser ones, have the potential to be mentors as well as friends. There are two valuable mentors in my life. Each of them has enriched my life beyond calculation. The first, a former business associate, taught me how to enjoy my life and my work. Before we became acquainted, I was much too serious for my own good. I needed to know how to lighten up, and he showed me.

My other great mentor lives here in my home village of Polperro. He is highly educated and worldly wise, and his command of English grammar is superior to mine. We meet for a jovial drink and a chat most Thursday evenings and he is a terrific sounding board for the ideas behind my books. He is not afraid to criticise and interrogate with a directness from which there is no hiding.

My writing is all the better for his interest because he brings to it a new perspective; he coaxes me into producing my best even if I do feel inclined to strangle him from time to time.

Typically, the ideal mentor to a person prone to depression is somebody who enjoys sharing his or her own ideas and who is both constructive and supportive, in addition to being a good, non-judgemental listener. Who do you know among your circle of friends and acquaintances who might be pleased and touched to discover you value them so highly that you would ask them for their assistance? When you have fully recovered from depression, you might wish to reciprocate his or her kindness by doing something similar for someone else.

51

Laughter

The world is a looking-glass, and gives back to every man the reflection of his own face. Frown at it, and it will in turn look sourly upon you; laugh at it and with it, and it is a jolly, kind companion.

William Makepeace Thackeray (1811–63),
Vanity Fair

Laugh and the world laughs with you; laugh and depression is in retreat.

Healthy young children laugh as many as four hundred times a day, the average adult manages fewer than fifteen laughs daily, and the clinically depressed are hard pushed to manage one decent laugh all day. These figures are disappointing when you consider that a good laugh can defuse tension, relieve stress, elevate mood and draw the sting from the agonies of social embarrassment.

The mental and physical health benefits of humour are well documented in a public health study conducted by Dr Lee Berk in California. One hour of naturally induced laughter significantly lowers levels of the stress hormones cortisol and epinephrine and stimulates the body's cells and antibodies.

Years ago, long before the first of my two strokes, I remember reading a quite remarkable book by the American journalist, Norman Cousins, entitled *Anatomy of an Illness* (W.W. Norton, 1979). In it, he tells of his painful struggle with a life-threatening spinal condition. He knew, from personal experience, just about everything there was to know about pain and he was aware that laughter had the power to release the body's natural painkillers, endorphins, into the bloodstream. One weekend, when the pain was monumental, he checked into a hotel, complete with a suitcase full of *Candid Camera* and *Marx Brothers* videos, and proceeded to test the therapeutic benefits of laughter. Cousins discovered that five minutes of spontaneous laughter (not polite, not restrained) gave him up to two hours of pain relief. And, despite his chronic condition, he felt better about himself and life in general.

In order to successfully humour our away out of depression, we shall need a strategy to escape from the emotional trough in which many of us find ourselves from time to time. One way to achieve this is to create a secret inner world of fun and frivolity, just like we did as very young children.

All of us have to live in this less-than-ideal world and our inner environment is the only one over which we can exercise any real control. We can help ourselves to cope with the ups and downs of life by developing our own personal sense-of-humour trigger. Here's an easy way to go about it: the object of the exercise is to be able to see the funny side of every situation that might otherwise upset you. During the evening, or last thing at night, is the ideal time to do this exercise.

Loosen your clothes and take off your shoes, relax your body and let the events of the day fade away. Take three slow, deep breaths and recall a happy moment from your very early childhood. For a few blissful moments you are going to be a child again.

Consciously force yourself to bring a smile to your face and summon the child from within you. Recall an incident from today that has (or could have) upset you and become, once again, the child you once were. Call on the child within you to poke fun at the incident in question. Change the facts of the matter and the ending to please yourself, just as if you were writing your own novel. Give it a funny ending, one that pleases you and makes you laugh.

52

Food for thought

Tell me what you eat: I will tell you what you are.

Jean-Anthelme Brillat-Savarin (1755–1826),
The Physiology of Taste

Minor changes in your eating habits can lead to major improvements in your
mental and physical health.

What you eat on a regular basis not only affects your day-to-day health, it can be instrumental in determining the quality of your life later on, how long you will live and whether or not you will become prone to illness and depression. Sadly, just when a balanced, wholesome diet is of prime importance, many people in the grip of depressive illness neglect their nutritional needs.

Some depressed people find they have very little appetite for food at all, while others go on binges or develop cravings for carbohydrates. As a result, many of us who are depressed may suffer from nutritional deficiencies or imbalances – particularly a lack of B vitamins and vitamin C, together with a shortage of the essential minerals: calcium, copper, iron, magnesium and potassium.

To combat a lack of B vitamins, speak to your pharmacist. My personal favourite is a tonic called Effico, which is effective and less expensive than other remedies.

The finest way to correct a deficiency of vitamin C is to get stuck into some exotic fruits, together with some really juicy, fresh oranges. For some strange reason, oranges, tangerines and mandarins seem to have the added bonus of turning me off chocolate, which is a major plus because chocolate is the last thing you should gorge when depressed.

Nutritional guidelines from the Department of Health offer pointers for sufferers of depression: plenty of wholegrains and pulses and regular amounts of lean meat, oily fish, shellfish and eggs will supply B vitamins, iron, potassium, magnesium, copper and zinc. A high intake of fresh fruit and vegetables (such as asparagus, broccoli, cabbage, melons, berries and oranges) will supply vitamin C in abundance. Dark-green leafy vegetables will increase levels of calcium, magnesium and iron; dried fruit will provide potassium and iron, while low-fat dairy produce will further boost reserves of calcium.

Overdosing on caffeine (more than four cups of coffee or six cups of tea a day) can exacerbate depression because caffeine can have the effect of contributing to sleeplessness. Readers should be aware that symptoms of caffeine withdrawal – headaches and lethargy – can last up to a maximum of three days before the full benefits of caffeine withdrawal can be enjoyed.

Eat your way healthily out of depression

- Consume more wholegrain breads and cereals such as barley, cracked wheat and oats. Choose brown bread in preference to white.
- Include more peas, beans and lentils in your diet. Foods derived from soybeans can be particularly beneficial.
- Eat at least five servings of fruit and vegetables daily.
- Include oily fish at least twice a week, e.g. salmon, mackerel and sardines.
- Minimise saturated fats, which can contribute to high cholesterol levels. The main offenders are: full-fat milk, cheese and creams, ice cream, processed meats, takeaways and crisps.
- Use low-fat dairy products whenever possible and, provided you don't have an allergy to nuts, include them (unsalted) in your diet. Nuts contain a very favourable mix of fatty acids, which can have a positive effect on blood fat levels.
- Reduce your alcohol intake, if applicable, to no more than one or two drinks a day.
- Try reducing salt intake by cutting back on pre-prepared soups, gravies, stock cubes, bacon, sausages, takeaways, pickles and crisps. Cut down or eliminate the unhealthy habit of sprinkling table salt on food. Salt has its place in the kitchen during the preparation and cooking of food. It is a health hazard in the dining room and does little for the real taste of food when it has already been served on the plate.

53

The default settings
of your mind

We know what we are, but know not what we may be.

William Shakespeare (1564–1616),
Hamlet

One little change of mind can unlock the deadlock.

Now is a convenient time to return to a familiar theme of mine: the analogy between the human mind and a computer. For the benefit of those who are not computer buffs (which, incidentally, includes most of us), I should point out that if you tell a computer to do something it will continue to do it until you tell it otherwise. For instance, if the setting on your computer is preset to leave two spaces after a full stop, that is what you will get unless it is specifically altered to leave only one space.

One can parallel this with the mind of a depressed person – their tendency will be to follow the same pattern of thought and not be capable of lifting themselves out of depression. Their pattern of outmoded (negative) thinking must be replaced by a revised way of thinking which will lead them to recovery. In other words, the 'default' setting in the mind must be altered to allow you to make progress.

To achieve this, it will be necessary to switch from outmoded to revised thinking at the birth of our thoughts, at the very moment they enter our conscious awareness. That is what we shall be doing in the next two chapters and it will not be difficult. In fact, it may even be rather fun.

54

D-thoughts

Great thoughts come from the heart.

Marquis de Vauvenargues (1715–47)

Defuse D-thoughts. D-thoughts are depressing thoughts.

Before we successfully adopt and benefit from a concept different to the one we are accustomed to, I find it helps to first know what *not to do*. With revised thinking, the concept by which you are going to banish depression and bring laughter, happiness and opportunity into your life, it is crucial to defuse D-thoughts! D-thoughts are dangerous thoughts, and we don't want any more of them.

Not only are D-thoughts dismal, dangerous and depressing, they are disabling as well because they drain you of the power to choose today how you will feel. For instance, if you lose your job, you could succumb to a wave of D-thoughts and despair at the prospect of ever getting another job. This is natural but the important thing is to move forward to the position where you can regard this enforced change as an opportunity to get a better job, downshift, or start an enterprise of your own.

The essential difference between these two thought patterns – the one, outmoded thinking and the other, revised thinking – is the absence of D-thoughts: the self-deprecating thoughts that immediately spring to mind if you let them.

D-thoughts should not be confused with the irritation and disappointment we feel when things go wrong, or the natural grieving process we experience over the death of a loved one. D-thoughts are an entrapment of mind born of habit in hard or threatening times and they lead us into a crisis of despair and hopelessness. They condition us to expect the worst and we must learn to stifle them at birth so that they cannot drag us down into depression and keep us there. We will find out how to do this in the next chapter but, first, let's see just how destructive D-thoughts can be . . .

According to a study published in the *British Journal of Psychiatry* in November 2000, the death of Princess Diana caused an alarming increase in the suicide rate throughout England and Wales. The increase was especially high among young women. Analysis of official government figures has revealed that the suicide rate jumped by almost a fifth (17.4 per cent) in the four weeks following her funeral.

The researchers, led by Professor Keith Hawton of the Warneford Hospital, Oxford, also found that cases of attempted suicide, including drug overdoses and other deliberate means of self-harm, increased by 44 per cent the week after Diana's death, with hospital admissions of women up a staggering 65 per cent.

The main contributing factor in almost all depressive illnesses and suicides is negative thinking – D-thoughts! In the next chapter there is a technique for defusing D-thoughts that anyone, from a child to a pensioner, can get to grips with. You are about to revise the default setting for your mind and to reach for recovery.

55

The revised setting for peace of mind

Great emergencies and crises show us how much greater our vital resources are than we had supposed.

William James (1842–1910)

It's time to switch from outmoded thinking to revised thinking.

Ivan Petrovich Pavlov (1849–1936), who received a Nobel Prize for his work on the digestive system and conditioned reflexes, is the Russian physiologist who is going to help me to make the concept of revised thinking supremely easy for you to understand.

The most famous of Pavlov's experiments were his studies on the behaviour of dogs. He would ring a bell and then feed the dogs. He repeated this procedure many times over a period of weeks: he rang the bell; the dogs salivated and ate the food. After a time, the dogs would salivate at the sound of the bell – even when no food was available. He described their response to the bell as a conditioned reflex: bell, salivation, food.

This type of reaction – responding instantaneously to a stimulus – became known as the 'Pavlovian response' and it was the source of Pavlov's insights into human behaviour. Our basic human thought processes, Pavlov found, work in much the same way and this is why it is sometimes necessary to revise the default settings of our minds, that is to say, the stimuli that set us off on the wrong track.

When we hear the bell, we don't want to salivate when no food is forthcoming. Likewise, we do not want to think the worst when the worst is not necessarily the only thing on offer. Sadly, many of us have unconsciously conditioned ourselves in depression to do just that, ignoring all other happier options by default.

As humans we can make ourselves aware that such stimuli are false, that we do not have to make the conditioned response. We can be aware of falling into the D-thought trap and turn away from it.

Our perceptions determine what we actually experience in any given situation because they make us receptive to some stimuli and blind to others. Those of us who expect to find problems in a given situation are usually able to find them, while those of us who expect to find opportunities in the same situation will also be successful. In order to revise the default setting of your mind from unhelpful D-thoughts to positive, forward-looking thinking, I am going to ask you to do three things. The code name I use for the process you are about to undertake is SS30.

SS30

1. Stop! Every time you catch yourself thinking a negative, depression-inducing D-thought, you should dismiss that thought immediately from your mind by thinking of Pavlov's dogs salivating at the mouth, before switching your thoughts to something good, satisfying and positively in your favour. Your revised thought can be any nice thought you please: a fond or happy memory from the past or a promising thought about the future, but absolutely no D-thoughts of any kind! For example, if you need help but find it difficult to ask for help, *think* how you feel when someone asks for your help and you give it. You feel good, don't you?

2. Suspend any disbelief in the effectiveness of this process for a period of thirty days. Please do exactly as I ask, even if you feel far from optimistic about the outcome right now. I want you to get well and I know you can do it.

3. 30 days is how long it can take to make or break a habit or to revise the default setting of your mind. To be certain of success, you must keep on banishing D-thoughts from your mind every second of every minute of every waking hour for thirty days. Don't worry; it becomes easier by the day! Very soon you will be a revised thinker. You will have succeeded in resetting the default setting of your mind and you will beat depression.

56

A purpose in life

Nothing contributes so much to tranquillise the mind as a steady purpose: a point on which the soul may fix its intellectual eye.

Mary Shelley (1797–1851)

For the vast majority of readers, destiny is not a matter of chance, *it is a matter of choice.*

Money, power, total freedom, a huge and impressive home, the hunkiest, most handsome man imaginable to satisfy your every whim or the queen of the catwalks as your personal trophy. If you had all that, and more, could you guarantee to be free of depression? Actually, no.

How do I know? The times in my life when I have experienced real satisfaction, success and fulfilment, have been, without exception, those times when I have followed my dream and set about doing what I had a genuine passion for. You should first subject whatever it is that you believe will bring purpose and meaning to your life in the future to the love test.

The love test? When considering your vocation, your purpose, your genuine passion for the game of life in which you are none other than the most important player, you must want to do it for the sheer joy of doing it, not just for the material benefits that you might reasonably expect it to provide. If your passion does not survive this crucial test, you could be mistaken in your assumption of what it is that will bring joy and happiness into your life. You may need to get more closely in touch with your inner self to realise your true destiny and to bring your dream to fruition.

The kiss in the tail of the love test, I have discovered, is that once you discover your real passion in life and go for it with persistence and determination, satisfaction comes eventually and then just keeps on coming. What's more, because you are doing what you love doing, not only is your life meaningful, happy and fulfilled, but your relationships and your interaction with loved ones become more natural and pleasing.

I could have written this book solely for the sheer enchantment and challenge of doing it, and the same applies to my first book, *After Stroke*, which in fact I wrote to give myself a reason to learn to read and comprehend the meaning of words again following the ravages of stroke illness (and, incidentally, as my way out of depression). I had no idea at the time that Thorsons would publish it on both sides of the Atlantic as an international paperback. The moral behind this and countless other success stories, similar and more spectacular, is to find your passion, that special something that means so much to you that you would willingly do it without payment – and the good things in life will then find you.

Only you can discover your purpose in life, which, for some

people, may be a variation or renewed intensity on something they are already doing, something completely different, or something they had always wanted to do but never quite dared to attempt until now. Once you have decided on the new direction or the new emphasis for your life, put it to the love test and if it passes, don't be surprised if your depression fades as you plan for action.

57

Committing your purpose to paper

I felt as if I were walking with destiny, and that my past life had been but a preparation for this hour and this trial . . . I was sure I should not fail.

Winston Churchill (1874–1965)

Write it down, read it regularly.

Before you can plan for action and expect to succeed it is a good idea to commit your new or renewed purpose in life to paper. In stress management and motivational jargon this is referred to as a 'personal mission statement'.

Life has more meaning and depth to it when we have something definite to do – a mission to fulfil – and if we fail to recognise this we run the risk of getting lost and becoming depressed should we experience bad luck, disappointment, something new that we are ill-equipped to deal with, or tragedy of any kind. By our very nature, our lives need to be dedicated to something and a crystal-clear mission statement, written from the heart and read regularly, helps to focus our mind.

If you spend your life doing what you really love doing, it stands to reason that life will be a pleasure and you will excel at what you do because you love doing it. This doesn't, of course, mean that every aspect of your life will be perfect, or even enjoyable, but it does mean that the general thrust of your life will be forward-looking, happy and fulfilling.

Many people start off with a passion for life but they lose it along the way. Perhaps you once had a passion for doing excellent work, taking risks, being creative, making friends, helping people, homemaking, childminding, theatre, exploring new ideas or possibilities or doing voluntary work for charity? Or perhaps you may have had a passion for the quiet life, or perhaps a zest for the cut and thrust of business, entertainment, adventure and travel that turned out to be less fulfilling than expected. Our priorities and passions change as we progress through life and in any event, we don't always get it right first time. I know I didn't.

Don't set out to impress yourself or anyone else with your personal mission statement. This really is your life you are going to forecast and the all-important ingredients of this statement are truth, realism and personal integrity. Whether you are sixteen years old or a hundred and six, the document you are about to prepare for your own exclusive use is of paramount importance to your future happiness.

So potentially rewarding for you is the next step, that I am about to break the rule of a lifetime. Never before have I shown my personal mission statement to anyone other than my fiancée and my mentor, but I am willing to put it before you now in the hope that it may inspire you to reach into your heart as never before and help you to prepare your own statement. Forget about all past mistakes and disasters. Get this right, and you will live a dream come true.

David M. Hinds
My Life in the Year 2000 and Beyond

I am creative and I will write some more really useful health and motivational books. I am doing this with my life because I want to and because I get tremendous satisfaction from the results of my writing. I regard the letters of appreciation from readers that are forwarded on to me by my publishers as a measure of my success. I am happy and enthused by this, my third and final career.

This year I will endeavour to find someone to love and cherish who is uniquely desirable: someone who will love me for ever and be happy living here in Polperro. I will be truthful, kind and faithful to her and we will be friends as well as lovers and lifelong partners.

The above mission statement, devised in the closing months of 1999, is already bearing fruit. This, my latest book, is due for publication in the summer of 2001, around the time of my marriage to Tatiana, the lovely lady to whom this book is dedicated. Why not make today the day you make a start on the next chapter of your life?

One of the great joys of my life at the present time is that one day a week I work exclusively with private clients throughout the UK, masterminding their comeback from depression and giving personal advice and assistance with their individual mission statements. Further information on this inititative can be obtained from The Comeback Consultancy, listed in the sources of help and support at the back of the book.

58

Adventure at any age

What you can do is limited only by what you can dream.

Dick Rutan, (1938—),
Voyager pilot

Some people believe we have many lives and that this one is merely for practice purposes. Religious people believe they will go to heaven. I believe we get only one innings and everyone owes it to himself or herself to find out how to make it as worthwhile and enjoyable as possible.

We are never too old to get it right and even if we do have another chance in another life, wouldn't it be nice to know we succeeded in turning our life on earth into a great adventure? We don't need money to achieve this; all we need is a sense of adventure.

Your life has the potential to be a wondrous journey, filled with exciting moments and astonishing experiences. It can be thrilling and deeply satisfying only if you are keen to explore all that is available to you. It doesn't matter if your life has been misspent or a bore to date, what matters is the change for the better you are prepared to make as a direct result of reading this book. You have everything to gain: make the nightmare of depression a positive turning point in your life. This option is red-hot, enticing and open to you. Only you can slam the door by default, by doing nothing to please yourself.

Are you interested in taking up this option? Good, here's how to overcome one of the two remaining hurdles standing between you and your depression-free life of the future. Answer the following question: what is it that gives you real satisfaction? What makes you spark? If you don't know, but you are willing to find out, you could be in for an even greater adventure; you may need to try many things in order to find out what really does it for you!

An adventure is any experience that takes you beyond your comfort level. Adventures are different things to different people, but they are invariably experiences that make your blood race and your heart beat with anticipation as you expand beyond your perceived limitations as a human being. They enlarge your horizons and take you into new territory, on to more exciting and satisfying levels of life. At the same time they benefit your family and friends because you become a richer and more interesting person, more worldly wise, someone who it is a pleasure to be around.

What you choose to make of your life is exclusively up to you: you can either create an exciting life filled with wonder and adventure or stay huddled and safe, never experiencing the thrill of journeying outside your own private world with its in-built routine and limitations. A life devoid of adventure may be secure, but it is a life lacking in texture and colour, one that can give rise to feelings of boredom, emptiness and depression.

Living life to the full by realising our dreams and finding time for fun and adventure is something most of us could do if we were prepared to go beyond our comfort zone. Depressed people have a distinct advantage over others in this respect. They have experienced so much pain, isolation and misery in the depths of their depressive illness that the prospect of change no longer looms like a potential nightmare to them; it is salvation: something to be embraced with open arms.

All that now remains is for you to decide what it is you want to do, what kind of thrill are you going to give your well-deserving self? Will it be an adventure with the potential to be highly therapeutic, like the one in the next chapter, or will you choose something completely different? Now that you are approaching the final hurdle, all that remains is for you to leap, lurch or launch yourself into action.

59

Swimming with dolphins

The day I swam with dolphins, I believe I was reborn.

Bill Bowell (1935—)

An unlikely new water therapy – swimming with dolphins – is proving remarkably effective in treating psychological illness. Horace Dobbs, founder of the Oxford Underwater Research Group, director of International Dolphin Watch and a former atomic scientist, reveals in his book *Dolphin Healing* (Piatkus, 2000), that interacting with dolphins can have a therapeutic effect on those suffering from depression. 'A dolphin can communicate moods that we can't define scientifically,' explains Dr Dobbs. 'One of the reasons why I believe humans have this special relationship with dolphins is that, in us, they recognise their cerebral partners. Dolphins rely on two senses, sound and vision, both of which are many times more complex than the human equivalent. They have the ability to carry out ultrasonic scans in their brains, which makes them highly sensitive to human emotions.'

Researchers have discovered that some dolphins break away from their habitual groups to become what scientists have described as 'ambassador' dolphins. These creatures are usually bottle-nosed dolphins and predominantly male. They live alone in their chosen territory and appear to prefer the company of humans. It is these dolphins, the evidence suggests, that have the ability to heal mental diseases. They have been described by sufferers and researchers alike as having telepathic skills for understanding and unlocking emotions and fears buried deep in the sufferer's mind.

A wealth of anecdotal evidence, as well as scientific studies, confirms the healing power of dolphins. Bill Bowell, a retired 65-year-old manager from Oxford, had suffered from chronic depression for years after having a heart attack at the age of fifty-three.

'Depression is such a devastating disease both for the sufferer and for the family,' he said. 'I was unable to work for twelve years because of it. I was a recluse, paranoid, aggressive and suffered from self-loathing. Doctors put me on several antidepressants over the years and I was assigned to psychiatric counselling, but nothing worked for me.'

Three years ago, Bill was lowered into the freezing waters of St Bride's Bay, off Solva in South Wales. 'My life changed for ever. I was petrified. I could barely swim and I was shaking like a leaf as the grey shape of a dolphin approached me from below.

'After I spotted him, he slowly crept up and lay beside me in the water. He looked straight into my eyes for a few minutes, and I burst into tears. I was mesmerised and my emotions erupted like a volcano. As I cried, he rested his head on my chest and stayed very still. Finally, after ten minutes, I reached out and touched him. He nudged my face and tickled my ribs until I laughed out loud.

'It was a moving experience and one I will never forget. Since then I have swum with dolphins on several occasions. I am now fully recovered: I take no medication and have returned to work. I am finally able to talk to my children again after almost ten years of barely knowing who they were.'

There are countless other stories from people who claim to have been healed after swimming with dolphins and there are many reliable ambassador dolphin territories around the world. The nearest operational location to the UK at the time of writing is at Dingle Bay in the Republic of Ireland (this activity is unavailable at St Bride's Bay at present).

Could this be a worthwhile adventure for you?

60

Downshifting

Take time to deliberate, but when the time for action has arrived, stop thinking and jump in.

Napoleon Bonaparte (1769–1821)

Do as you wish with your one and only life.

At one time in my life, before my strokes, I was the chairman and chief executive of a UK plc group with ninety-two stress management consultancies. Since recovering from my illness, I have written two books. No staff, no company headquarters, just me.

Although to a great extent my change of circumstances was dictated by misfortune, I am happier and more contented with my lifestyle now. Mine is a classic example of downshifting. No more the impressive fifteen-room bachelor house with stables. These days I live in a small but pleasant flat overlooking a river. Given a choice between my two lifestyles, past and present, complete with all those special little 'extras' and benefits, which would I choose? No contest! I would choose to live simply as I do now.

Money, power and success are great but they cannot buy love, happiness and contentment. These days, I have all three. I highly recommend downshifting for those who wish to enjoy the quality of their lives.

Almost everyone has a fantasy that one day they will win a National Lottery and this will give them everything they have ever yearned for in life. The mere prospect appears so enchanting that hundreds of millions of people around the world sit glued to their TV sets every week watching the winning balls drop. In that moment of suspense they glimpse the possibility of a future devoid of all problems: one filled with luxury and joy.

Sadly, the real-life recipe for financial bliss is not so idyllic. Happiness guru Professor Michael Argyll of Oxford Brookes University, UK, maintains that once your income is roughly average for the society you are living in, simply having more money will not make you happier in the foreseeable future. The ability to spend with gay abandon gives you a short-term buzz, of course, but it provides very little long-term satisfaction. So many intelligent, hard-working men and women blind themselves to this essential truth. They strive to earn more and more and then fall into the money-fleecing traps ingeniously laid by the advertising industry to relieve them of all they have earned.

In the more politically correct and gender-equal workplace of today, men are increasingly suffering from anxiety and depression because their female partners are offloading the pressures of their own jobs at the end of the working day. The growing professional demands on wives and girlfriends are rubbing off on their male partners, whose psyches are suffering as a result. In contrast, modern women are less likely to be bothered if their men are having a hard time at work because women these days are emotionally tougher and more in control, say researchers.

Do you find yourself saving less money and watching more TV; itching to buy more things, no matter how much you already possess; buying your children bigger and better presents instead of spending more quality time with them; wanting more, no matter how educated or successful you become? If you are depressed and you have answered 'yes' to one or more of these questions, perhaps downshifting could be a happier and healthier option for you and your family.

For many, the dream of 'having it all' has turned sour. The material benefits have not yielded the expected satisfaction. As the pressures and insecurities of the rat race become ever more daunting, more and more people are opting for a better, simpler way of life: one that offers the prospect of greater happiness and more time to enjoy their families. Downshifting is coming of age.

61

Balance

Instead of seeing the rug being pulled from under us we can learn to dance on the shifting carpet.

Thomas F. Crum (1937—)

Balance, on the tightrope through life, requires flexibility.

Depression, however frightening, is never permanent. Nevertheless, it is wise to have it treated in order to spare yourself, your family and your friends needless pain and suffering, and to reduce the risk of suicide while the mind is unbalanced. Whether it is treated or not, depression has a tendency to disappear of its own accord. This may take a few weeks, months or well over a year, but it invariably happens. Our brain chemistry adjusts to the imbalance in the system and corrects itself – until the next time – but we ourselves can learn to get some genuine balance into our lives.

Our brains seldom tolerate extremes of emotion for long periods. Just remember the ecstasy of those heady, early days in love. You felt as though you were floating on air, unable to eat, concentrate, or think of anything but the object of your emotions. Did it last? You may well still be in love with that wonderful person but you won't be on such a high. The endorphins, which our brains create to make us feel wonderful at the birth of new love, overload, then balance out over time. Fortunately, a not dissimilar balancing act takes place in the reverse, lifting us from depression.

Lasting happiness, emotional wellbeing, and the ability to remain permanently free of depression are internal processes which are generated from within each of us. Only we can decide how best to live our lives and exactly what personal fulfilment means to each of us.

The thrust of this book has been a common sense approach to beating depression once and for all by taking full responsibility for our thoughts, our lives, our decisions, our behaviour and our mistakes. There is no mileage in the blame game any more. We have learned how damaging and self-defeating that spiteful little boomerang can be. Instead of blaming others and ourselves for any shortcomings we may have, we are going to set about getting some real balance into our lives.

Here are some suggestions as to how to go about it:

- When you are working, give it all you've got, but be sure to spend quality time with your loved ones and make some special time available exclusively for you to do the things that you want to do.
- Live your life now. All time is real time. Don't put your life on hold waiting for a more convenient time to live it.

- Consider how much time you spend surfing the Internet, watching TV and drinking in pubs. Relaxation is important, of course, but are you doing these things to relax or because you're lonely or bored?
- If you don't like your life, or if there are aspects of it that don't appeal, make a list of the pluses and minuses in your lifestyle and set about making a plan to improve things.
- The key to a balanced life is spending sufficient time on the various components of your life: career, family, health, pursuits and hobbies, social aspects, further education, belief structures, leisure, holidays, entertainment, community affairs and charity work, etc.
- Be friendly and forgiving to those around you. Friendship is a goal worth pursuing. It means you can find a way to meet in the middle and share other people's dreams without feeling as if you are sacrificing anything. There is something very special about true friendship, something worth cultivating.
- Refer to the personal mission statement you prepared in Chapter Fifty-seven, amend it if necessary, and set about thinking of ways to make it happen.
- Ask yourself, 'What do I wish I had more time for?' Make it happen!
- Once in a while, do something nice, spontaneous, unexpected and totally out of character, for someone else. *Get some excitement back into life!*

62

Enjoying the moment

Happy the man, and happy he alone,
He, who can call to-day his own:
He who, secure within, can say,
To-morrow do thy worst, for I have lived to-day.

John Dryden (1631–1700),
From a translation of Horace, 65–8 BC

Look until you find something promising in your situation.

Eventually, when you look back on your life, it's unlikely that you will be thinking about how much money you did or didn't make, or whether or not you got your own back on that person who crossed you. You are more likely to be thinking about the purpose of your life and the people in it who mean so much to you.

We all change as we journey through life. There was a time when I used to think that all that mattered was success and making a fortune. These days, I believe the purpose of life is to *live*, love and be loved and, in some small way, to enrich the lives of others. If your life doesn't strike you as worthwhile or rewarding, change it: it is never too late to change.

On the assumption that you are not at death's door, indulge in life. Don't put off living it until you are feeling completely and utterly better. The experience of depression is awful, but you stand to gain so much from what you've been through when you decide to act upon the knowledge and greater understanding of yourself that you now possess.

Start doing some of the things that you always wanted to do. Make your life enjoyable and meaningful and others will benefit, too.

If you want to make things difficult for yourself, you'll find all the reasons in the world why you shouldn't enjoy your life: why you should postpone enjoyment until things are different, until you have got whatever it is you want. But time is ticking away and not one single moment can be replaced. The life you have lived so far has gone for ever. You can't have it back to relive those wasted moments.

The best any of us can do is to put greater value on life in future and to treasure all those remaining moments, including this one. The assumption that we will always have another moment, a moment better than this one, is flawed in one fatal respect: our lives can be changed completely in the twinkling of an eye by a heart attack, a motorway pile-up, or a stray bullet meant for someone else.

In the split second before I suffered a stroke in my late forties, had you asked me if I were going to be seriously ill for the next three years, I would have laughed in your face. Had you enquired a moment later, I would have been speechless. Enjoying the moment is the most wonderful concept you can adopt and it is your home-work for the rest of your life.

63

Highlighting

The farewell quotation

Some books are to be tasted, others to be swallowed,
and some few to be chewed and digested.

Francis Bacon (1561–1626)

Reach for your highlighting pen.

Let there be no doubt from the outset what this chapter is about. It is about extracting maximum benefit from this book by having a yellow (I suggest yellow, purely because it complements, rather than obscures, black print) highlighter pen to hand while you read, to highlight those words and paragraphs which may have particular significance for you. Why? So that you can locate them again quickly and easily, time and time again, whenever you need them for reinforcement and encouragement.

Why am I telling you this now, in the last chapter?

On the first page of this book, it required only one tick to involve you in your own recovery, but even if you were only mildly depressed, that tick was not only the first step, it was a *major* step towards recovery. I had no intention at that point of complicating matters with highlighters and re-reads.

Almost everyone reads a book, even a self-help book, as if it were a novel: from front to back, seldom stopping to question and re-read those sections with specific relevance to him or her. This is fine for a first read, but within these pages are techniques and strategies that have taken me over thirty years to extract from my experiences and evolve into book form. Even Superman could not be expected to absorb all this in one read.

From my experiences of successfully recovering from clinical depression and, in later years, treating depressed clients either as individuals in my stress management consultancies or as participants in my 'Tackling Under-Performance' workshops, I believe this book will succeed in its stated aim, but seriously depressed readers will need more than one casual read. *Hence the highlighter* . . .

Whenever I read a book that I am determined to benefit from, I devour it. I read each line again and again if necessary until I have fully grasped the meaning of every word, highlighting the passages that strike me as being of crucial importance.

To gain maximum benefit from this book, to attend to all of the issues leading up to your depression and to resolve them, you must do the same: devour this book; extract all the information that could be useful to you, and then set about translating the essential principles and strategies you have learned into *action*. Recovery may not be easy, instantaneous or swift, but it will happen.

Sources of help and support

United Kingdom

Age Concern
1268 London Road
London SW16 4ER

Telephone: 020 8679 8000

Alcoholics Anonymous
PO Box 1
Stonebow House
Stonebow
York YO1 2NJ

Telephone: 020 7833 0022 and 01904 644026

The Association for Postnatal Illness
25 Jerdan Place
Fulham
London SW6 1BE

Telephone: 020 7386 0868

Beat Depression clubs and **Tackling Under-Performance workshops** for companies in association with the author
Brackenside House
4 Brackenside Lane
Polperro
Cornwall PL13 2RU

E-mail: davidhindsauthor@beatdepression.fslife.co.uk
Website: www.beatdepression.fslife.co.uk

Black and Asian Mental Health Resource Centre
Bushberry House
4 Laurel Mount
St Mary's Road
Leeds LS7 3JX

Telephone: 0113 237 4229

Carers National Association
20–25 Glasshouse Yard
London EC1A 4JS

Telephone: 020 7490 8818

Childline (free counselling and advice exclusively for children – depressed or not!)
Freepost 1111
London N1 0BR

Telephone: 0800 1111 (helpline); 020 7239 1000 (admin)

The Comeback Consultancy
16 Hills View
Langreek
Looe
Cornwall PL13 2PN

Telephone: 01503 273074 and 01503 273079

CRUISE – Bereavement Care
126 Sheen Road
Richmond
Surrey TW9 1UR

Telephone: 020 8332 7227

Depression Alliance
35 Westminster Bridge Road
London SE1 7JB

Telephone: 020 7633 0557
Website: www.depressionalliance.org

Depression Alliance Cymru
11 Plas Melin Westbourne Road
Whitchurch
Cardiff CF4 2BT

Telephone: 029 2069 2891

Depression Alliance Scotland
3 Grosvenor Gardens
Edinburgh EH12 5JU

Telephone: 0131 467 3050

Down's Syndrome Association
155 Mitham Road
Tooting
London SW17 9PG

Telephone: 020 8682 4001

Help the Aged
16–18 St James's Walk
London EC1R 0BE

Telephone: 020 7253 0253

Lundbeck Award for Good Medical Practice in Depression
Depression Alliance
Freepost LON 1076
PO Box 1022
London SE1 7UX

Telephone: 020 7633 0557

Manic Depression Fellowship
Castle Works
21 St George's Road
London SE1 6ES

National advice line: 020 7793 2600
Scotland advice line: 0141 400 1867
Wales advice line: 01633 244 244
E-mail: mdf@mdf.org.uk
Website: www.mdf.org.uk

Meet-a-Mum Association
26 Avenue Road
London SE25 4DX

Telephone: 020 8771 5595

National Association for Mental Health (MIND)
Granta House
15–19 Broadway
Stratford
London E15 4BQ

Telephone: 020 8519 2122
National information line: 0345 660 163
E-mail: email@mind.org.uk
Website: www.mind.org.uk

The National Childbirth Trust
Alexandra House
Oldham Terrace
Acton
London W3 6NH

Telephone: 020 8992 8637

National Schizophrenia Fellowship (NSF)
28 Castle Street
Kingston upon Thames
Surrey KT1 1SS

Telephone: 020 8974 6814 (advice); 020 8547 3937 (admin)

National Schizophrenia Fellowship (NSF) Scotland
40 Shandwick Place
Edinburgh EH2 4RT

Telephone: 0131 226 2025

Northern Ireland Association for Mental Health
Beacon House
80 University Street
Belfast BT7 1HE

Telephone: 01232 328474

Relate (formerly the Marriage Guidance Council)
Herbert Gray College
Little Church Street
Rugby CV21 3AP

Telephone: 01788 573241

The Royal College of Psychiatrists
17 Belgrave Square
London SW1X 8PG

Telephone: 020 7235 2351 (ext 259)
Website: www.rcpsych.ac.uk

The Samaritans
10 The Grove
Slough SL1 1QP

Telephone: 08457 909090 (National helpline); 01753 216500 (admin)
Fax: 01753 775787
E-mail: jo@samaritans.org
Website: http:www.samaritans.org.uk

Scottish Association for Mental Health
Cumbrae House
15 Carlton Court
Glasgow G5 9JP

Telephone: 0141 568 7000
E-mail: enquiries@samh.org.uk

Seasonal Affective Disorder Association (SADA)
PO Box 989
Steyning
W. Sussex BN44 3HG

Telephone: 01903 814942

Republic of Ireland

Aware – Helping to Defeat Depression
72 Lower Leeson Street
Dublin 2

Telephone: 01 8308449 (admin); 01 676616 (National helpline)

The Mental Health Association of Ireland
Mensana House
6 Adelaide Street
Dun Laoghaire
Co. Dublin

Telephone: 01 2841166
E-mail: info@mensana.org

The Samaritans
10 The Grove
Slough SL1 1QP
UK

Telephone: 1850 60 90 90 (National helpline/Eire)
E-mail: jo@samaritans.org
Website: www.samaritans.org.uk

United States of America

American Academy of Child and Adolescent Psychiatry
3615 Wisconsin Avenue, N.W.
Washington, DC 20016

Telephone: (202) 966–7300
Electronic bulletin board (dial from computer): 1–800–333–7636
Website: www.aacap.org

American Psychiatric Association
Division of Public Affairs
1400 K Street, N.W.
Washington, DC 20005

Telephone: (202) 682–6142
E-mail: m.bennet@apa.org
Website: www.psych.org

American Psychological Association
750 First Street, N.E.
Washington, DC 20002–4242

Telephone: (202) 336–5700
Website: www.apa.org

Association for the Care of Children's Health
7910 Woodmont Avenue
Suite 300
Bethesda, MD 20814

Telephone: (301) 654–6549
Electronic bulletin board: 1–800–808–2224
E-mail: acch@clark.net
Website: www.wsd.com/acch.org

Center for Mental Health Services' Knowledge Exchange Network
PO Box 42490
Washington, DC 20015

Telephone: 1–800–789–2647
Electronic bulletin board: 1–800–790–2647

Children and Adults with Attention Deficit Disorder (CH.A.D.D.)
499 Northwest 70th Avenue
Suite 101
Plantation, FL 33317

Telephone: (954) 587–3700
Electronic bulletin board: 1–800–233–4050
E-mail: majordomo@mv.mv.com

Children's Rights of America
8735 Dunwoody Place
Suite 6
Atlanta, GA 30350

Telephone: (770) 998–6698
Operates the National Youth Crisis Hotline: 1–800–442–4673 (a 24-hour emergency number for kids who are suicidal, being abused, etc.)

Federation of Families for Children's Mental Health
1021 Prince Street
Alexandria, VA 22314

Telephone: (703) 684–7710
E-mail: ffcmh@crosslink.com

Maternal and Child Health Bureau
Health Resources and Services Administration
Public Health Services
5600 Fishers Lane
Rockville, MD 20857

Telephone: (301) 443–0205
Website: www.os.dhhs.gov/hrsa/mchb

National Alliance for Research on Schizophrenia and Depression
60 Cutter Mill Road
Suite 404
Great Neck, NY 11021

Telephone: (516) 829–0091
Electronic bulletin board: 1–800–829–8289
Website: www.mhsource.com

National Committee to Prevent Child Abuse (NCPCA)
PO Box 2866
Chicago, IL 60690

Telephone: (312) 663–3520
Electronic bulletin board: 1–800–55–NCPCA
Website: www.childabuse.org

National Depressive and Manic Depressive Association (NDMDA)
730 North Franklin
Suite 501
Chicago, IL 60610

Telephone: (312) 652–0049
Electronic bulletin board: 1–800–826–3632 (1–800–82–NDMDA)

National Foundation for Depressive Illness
PO Box 2257
New York, NY 10016–2257

Telephone: 1–800–248–4344 (for recorded announcement)

National Institute of Mental Health (NIMH)
Depression Awareness, Recognition and Treatment Program
(DART)
Dept. GL, Room 10–85
5600 Fishers Lane
Rockville, MD 20857

Telephone: (301) 443–4140
Electronic bulletin board: 1–800–421–4211

National Mental Health Association (NMHA)
National Public Education Campaign on Clinical Depression
1021 Prince Street
Alexandria, VA 22314–2971

Telephone: (703) 684–7722
Electronic bulletin board: 1–800–969–6642
Website: www.worldcorp.com/dc-online/nhm

Canada

Alberta

Canadian Mental Health Association (CMHA)
328 Capital Place, 9707–110th St.
Edmonton, AB T5K 2L9

Telephone: (780) 482–6576

Depression and Manic-Depression Association of Alberta
Box 64064
Edmonton, AB T5H 0X0

Telephone: 1–888–757–7077

British Columbia

CMHA
#1200–1111 Melville St.
Vancouver, BC V6E 3V6

Telephone: (604) 688–3234

Mood Disorders Association of British Columbia
201–2730 Commercial Dr.
Vancouver, BC V5N 5P4

Telephone: (604) 873–0103

Manitoba

CMHA
2–836 Ellice Ave.
Winnipeg, MB R3G 0C2

Telephone: (204) 775–8888

Mood Disorders Association of Manitoba
4–1000 Notre Dame Ave.
Winnipeg, MB R3E 0N3

Telephone: (204) 786–0987

New Brunswick

CMHA
65 Brunswick St.
Fredericton, NB E3B 1G5

Telephone: (506) 455–5231

Newfoundland

CMHA
Box 5788
St John's, NF AIC 5X3

Telephone: (709) 753–8550

Northwest Territories

CMHA
PO Box 2580
Yellowknife, NT X1A 2P9

Telephone: (867) 873–3190

Nova Scotia

CMHA
63 King St.
Dartmouth, NS B2Y 2R7

Telephone: (902) 466–6600

Ontario

CMHA
180 Dundas St. W.
Suite 2301
Toronto, ON M5G 1Z8

Telephone: (416) 977–5580

Mood Disorders Association of Ontario
40 Orchard View Blvd.
Suite 222
Toronto, ON M4R 1B9

Telephone: (416) 486–8046

Prince Edward Island

CMHA
178 Fitzroy St., PO Box 785
Charlottetown, PEI C1A 7L9

Telephone: (902) 566–3034

Quebec

CMHA
550 Sherbrooke St. W.
Suite 2075
Montreal, QC H3A 1B9

Telephone: (514) 849–3291

L'Association des dépressifs et maniaco-dépressifs
801, rue Sherbrooke est, bureau 301
Montréal, QC H2L 1K7

Telephone: (514) 529–7552

Saskatchewan

CMHA
2702 12th Ave.
Regina, SK S4T 1J2

Telephone: (306) 525–5601

Yukon

CMHA
6 Bates Cres.
Whitehorse, YK Y1A 4T8

Telephone: (867) 668–8812
Depression hotline: 1–888–557–5051

South Africa

The Befrienders Bloemfontein
PO Box 2201
Bloemfontein 9300

Telephone: 051–4483000

Befrienders Mitchell's Plain
PO Box 219
Mitchell's Plain 7789

Telephone: 021–3111481

Befrienders Setshabelo
PO Box 21115
Heidedal 9306

Telephone: 051–4303555

Befrienders Umkomaas
PO Box 10447
Umkomaas 4170

Telephone: 039–9795638

The South African Anxiety Disorders Support Group
PO Box 650301
Benmore 2010

Telephone: 11–884–1797
Tollfree helpline: 0800–11–8392 or 0800–11–9283

Australia

24–hour crisis helpline for kids anywhere in Australia
Telephone (for the cost of a local call): 1800–55–1800

Anti Depression Group
Hobart Narrative Centre
Corner of Burnett Street and Murray Street
North Hobart

Telephone: (03) 6231–6872

Befriender Service
160 New Town Road
New Town

Telephone: (03) 6228–0313

Community Support and Outreach Support
250 Liverpool Street
Hobart

Telephone: (03) 6231–1345

ESP Support – Early Support for Parents
McDougal 1 Building
Ellerslie Road
Hobart

Telephone: (03) 6223–2937

Mental Health Community Resource Centre
97 Campbell Street
Hobart

Telephone: (03) 9236–9286; Toll free: 1800–808–890

Panic Anxiety Disorders Association (PADAWA)
189 Royal Street
East Perth
Western Australia

Telephone: (08) 9380–9898

Queensland Manic Depressive Support Group
Mental Health Friendship House
20 Balfour Street
New Farm
Queensland

Telephone: (07) 358–4988

SANE Australia
PO Box 226
South Melbourne 3065

Telephone: (03) 9682–5933
E-mail: info@sane.org

Index